FOREX TRADING FOR BEGINNERS:

Simple Secret Strategies, Psychology Trick and Tips for Investing in Short- and Long-Term Currency Exchange. Earning a Living and Create a Passive Income from Home.

II

Introduction 1

Chapter 1: Forex Trading Pros and Cons 5

Chapter 2: Opening a Brokerage Account 17

Chapter 3: Currency Pairs and PIPS 27

Chapter 4: Fundamental and Technical Analysis ... 55

Chapter 5: Tools, Indicators, and Patterns of Trading 71

Chapter 6: Scalping Strategy 83

Chapter 7: What Are the Most Popular Forex Trading Styles and Strategies? 91

Chapter 8: A New Species, Cryptocurrency 109

Chapter 9: How to Develop a Winning Routine 117

Chapter 10: Manage Your Emotions with Trading Psychology 125

Chapter 11: Risk management & Trading Plan 137

Chapter 12: Common Mistakes and Tips for Beginners in Forex Trading 145

Conclusion 153

Introduction

Forex market is a market where you will buy, sell, exchange as well as speculate on the currencies. The market comprises of banks, retail forex brokers, hedge funds, central banks as well as investors. The currency market tends to be a financial market that has a tremendous amount of transaction, exceeding the combination of equity markets and futures. It is the most liquid of all the markets and the currencies traded against each other. Exchanging currencies is one of the most crucial things since that has to be there if people need to do foreign trade as well as business.

Despite being among the most significant market, there is no central place that the exchange takes place. All the transactions are done over-the-counter. The market is always open, and it is so in the entire world. You will find that the market is still active during day time and the price quotes change from time to time. The transactions will happen so that one can have a financial advantage. The fact that individual currency varies is what that will make the need for foreign exchange to raise.

When it comes to conducting trade, commercial as well as investment banks are in charge of doing that on their client's behalf. There are cases when individual and professional investors have the opportunity to trade in currency. But it is challenging for them, and it gives them a tough time. The internet has been a way that individual traders know more about the forex market.

For someone who is getting into the market for the first time, they will find it risky as well as complex to handle. There are different regulations, and there is standardization of the forex instruments. You can find cases where the market has no rules in some parts of the world. The banks that are in that trade will determine and be in a position to accept any risk that will come with the deal. They need to make sure that they are safe so that they will not suffer huge losses. That will be possible when they put an internal process in place. The bank will impose the regulations that it feels will work the best for them. The protection they require will be a determinant of the kind of riles that will put in place. Any bank that is willing to participate in the forex market will provide an offer and a particulars currency bid. The way they will determine the prices will depend on the demand that there is in the market and the amount they and afford to supply. The traders cannot manage to influence any prices because the system has large trade flow. The method is vital in terms of creating transparency, and the investors can have access to the interbank dealing.

When you are a small retail trader, you are likely to have brokers who are not regulated and will re-quote the prices any time they wish. In some cases, they will even trade against you and take advantage of you. There may be some regulations, but that will depend on the area that your dealer is. The rules are not consistent in the whole world. So that you will know whether a dealer is under regulation or not, you need to take a thorough investigation. When you do that, you will get to know even where they are regulated. Seek to see the kind of protections that are there in case a crisis arises or the dealer's insolvency.

I a trader and you want to get in the trade and have no enough funds, day trading or swing trading is a comfortable option. If you have no issues with the limitation of funds, you can get in carrying trade or long-term fundamental-based trade. That will give you maximum profit, and you will find it worth investing your time and energy in the deal. For you to have high yields, you need to have a focus and understand the macroeconomic principles that drive the currency value. You need to have an experience with the technical analysis so that you will not be subject to losses. Know that the historical price will play a significant role in determining future rates. There is enormous data that is available out there in the market since it is done during the day and the night. That data will be useful for you to be in a position to determine the price movement in the future. For traders that like to use the technical tool, they will thrive in this market.

The prices in the forex market have a quotation of four decimal places since they have spread differences that are naturally very small. That makes it impossible to have a definitive rule on the number of decimal places that will be in forex quotes. You need to consider the risk that will come along with the trade before you get into the real currency trade. The trade-in currency is likely to be conducted in pairs. The pairs need to have low volatility as well as high liquidity. They are stable, add has well-managed economies having low chances of manipulation and smaller spread compared to other pairs. Some pairs consist of currencies from a small economy and those from a significant economy

Forex trading works in a way that the likelihood of making a profit is higher than that of making losses. Apart from benefit, numerous advantages will favor you when you get into a currency trade. The advantages of the forex market include and not limited to.

Chapter 1:
Forex Trading Pros and Cons

Forex trading has many favorable aspects, but just like every other trading activity, it has a downside. Every trader that seeks to enter the trade system must assess the advantages and disadvantages of foreign exchange before they make a decision in the appropriateness and attractiveness of the market.

Advantages

Forex exchange has a large number of advantages regardless of the risks; therefore, it makes an attractive and lucrative activity.

The advantages include:

Leverage

Leverage provides traders with substantial opportunities for them to trade and make profits. Access to leverage largely determines the difference between small profits and large ones. In the foreign exchange market, there are more resources for leverage than other markets and depending on the location from which a trader is working from one can get the resource they need. A trader may be able to access a margin that supports leverage of 100:1 or more for the initial capital.

Fast returns

The foreign exchange market moves very fast, and the liquidity is very deep. When the speed, liquidity, and high leverage are combined in the forex market, they create great opportunities for the trader to make exponential profits in the trade more than other markets. In some other markets, the traders have to wait for very long and still get limited returns.

Easy "short selling"

In some other markets, short selling may require a trader to borrow assets and get exposed to risks, but in the forex exchange, short selling currencies have a simpler process. Foreign exchange works in a way that the trader buys one currency while selling the other. In other words, the currencies are traded in pairs. Traders speculate the inclines and declines of different currencies, therefore, sell the losing currency and buy the winning pair without involving a borrowing process.

Liquidity

Because the forex market is the largest market in the world by volume, there are many participants; therefore, liquidity for trading is ample especially for the major currencies. Liquidity allows the traders to buy and sell the currencies quickly at any time; there is a flow of traders in the market. A large number of participants in the market enable the trader to transact extremely large orders of currencies without diverting the prices too much. Liquidity reduces the chances of price anomalies and manipulation, and as such, the spreads become tighter leading to efficient pricing. A trader does not have to worry about the stagnant prices during the afternoon and high volatility during the opening and closing which constantly affect the equity markets. In the forex market, a trader can observe similarities in the patterns of volatility (low, mid and high) apart from times when major events occur.

Lack of central exchange

Keeping in mind that the forex exchange market operates globally, there is no central regulatory or centralized exchange. The market operates as an over the counter although central banks occasionally interfere with the operations as needed in order to regulate it. However, it is very rare for the central banks of any other authority to intervene unless under extreme conditions. The decentralization and deregulation of the market ensure that the traders are safe from sudden surprises. Many of the other security markets are centralized for example the equity market. When a company trading in the equity market suddenly reports losses or declares a dividend, the prices suddenly react to the information. Regulated markets also have higher chances of insider information compared to forex markets.

A variety of pairs to trade

There are eight major currencies traded in the forex market, and they result in 28 major currency pairs that one may choose from. A trader can select any pair and easily switch from one to the other.

Low-capital requirements

A trader can start trading in the forex market with a low amount of initial capital because of the tight spread in relation to pips. In some other markets, one may not be able to trade without a large amount of capital. To ice the low capital cake, forex exchange also has a margin trading and leverage factor.

Technical strategy

Many traders venturing into bonds and equity have to delve deep into the financial and fundamental state of the bonds or share issuer in order to confirm that there are chances of making a profit. However, the forex market, traders do not have to dig too deep, all they need is to study the price charts. Technical analysis of forex market price charts helps the traders identify their entry and exit points. However, they may choose to combine technical and fundamental analysis when selecting a trade.

While fundamental analysis requires one to get detailed background information about the assets of the issuer and the financial health and prospects, Technical analysis requires one to watch the trends and histories of the market, therefore, getting clues on the demands and supply of the currencies.

No insider price manipulation

Many markets such as stock markets and bond markets can be influenced by information held privately by some investors and insiders who have interests in the assets. This is because most of the markets are centralized. Foreign exchange markets are not centralized; therefore, they cannot be easily manipulated by people who have insider information.

In most cases, the only holders who can access insider information in the forex exchange are central bank authorities or government officials, and they are usually under a lot of intense scrutiny from the public and the private sectors. As such, the foreign exchange market is one of the most transparent markets one can trade in.

Few commissions and fees

Traders get charged Pricey commissions and hidden trading fees when dealing with bonds, equities mutual funds and other kinds of instruments. This makes trading very expensive and reduces the profits of the trader. In forex trade, the costs of trading are determined by the bid-ask price only. The spread price is the difference between the bid and the asking price which is clearly published in real time by the brokers. As such, a trader does not have to worry about eliminating breakage overheads. This aspect makes Forex exchange more advantageous to trade in.

Simple tax rules

In many other markets, the traders have to keep track of their trading activities both in the short term and the long term in order to report taxes. However Foreign exchange trading is in most cases subject to a simpler tax rule, therefore, making tax calculations very easy.

Automation

Technology advancements have made it easy for forex traders to trade with utmost ease. The trade has adapted well to automated trading strategies, and with some training, a trader can reap the benefits of the available moves. A trader can set up programming entry, automated trades, limit prices and stop loss before he/she even makes a trade. The trader may also instruct the trading platform to transact when there are certain price movements or market conditions.

When a trader identifies a well revised automated strategy, he/she may have the chance to take advantage of the daily swings in the market without having to put all their efforts in keeping up with the movements in the market.

Suits different trading styles

Trade in the forex market happens at all hours of the day, Monday to Friday, therefore, enabling a trader to work at their own convenience. This schedule is very beneficial especially for short term traders because they take positions over a limited timeframe (a few hours or even a few minutes.). Some traders prefer to trade during off hours. Off hours refer to the times when one trade zone is not so active, and the other is active. For example, when it is daytime in Australia, it is nighttime on the east coast of the United States. If a trader is based in the US, he may trade AUD during the business hours in the US because the prices are quite stable and little development is expected to occur during the off hours for UAD. The traders who prefer off hours trade adopt the strategies of high volumes and low profits because they have a little profit margin. The low-profit margin results from the lack of developments in the particular currency. Off hours traders, therefore, try to compensate the low-profit-margin with high volume trades during the low volatility period. Other trading styles allow the traders to hold positions for a longer time; days to several weeks.

Disadvantages

Although trading may appear easy at first sight, some challenges make it hard for the traders. In some cases, the challenges can have serious adverse effects on the trader.

Volatility

All markets show volatility at one point or another. The forex market is not excluded from volatility. Forex traders are exposed to volatilities at times, and if the effects are negative, the trade will be unprofitable.

Forex can disadvantage small traders

In a day, the foreign exchange market can transact up to but not limited to $5 trillion. That huge amount of transaction is usually done by the main layers such as hedge funds, banks, and other larger institutions. These major players have access to a lot of capital, technology and also information that might give them an upper hand while making decisions; therefore, they are naturally advantaged. To some extent, these major players can influence the movement of prices in the market.

On the other hand, a small trader will have to stay alert and utilize the latest information in the best way possible because the forex market is very fast moving. The reality of small traders being disadvantaged is evident in almost all markets, but the forex exchange market is highly affected.

The forex market is not regularized, and it is dominated by brokers. The fact that there are many brokers makes it hard to have full transparency. A trader is competing against professionals, and he/she may not have a say in how the trade order gets fulfilled. The trader may also not get a good price, and he/she will only have access to the quotes provided by the selected broker. The best course is to deal with the brokers who are under the broker regulators. Although the market is not regulated, the actions of the brokers are.

The complex process of price determination

The rates in the forex markets are determined by multiple factors such as global politics, economic status, among others. Some of these factors can pose challenges in analyzing and quantifying, therefore, a trader can have a hard time drawing reliable conclusions on the trade. To a large extent, forex trading relies on technical indicators (Mathematical calculations based on volume, price or open interest of securities). Technical analysts analyze historical data and use the indicators to predict the price movements in the future. If a trader gets the predictions wrong, he/she will incur losses.

Lighter regulatory protection

Many traders and investors have a list of securities they can choose to trade in, and they prefer to act on trades that are swift and have transparent pricing. For most well-known securities, trading takes place in on formal exchanges constituting of large institutions that set the regulations and are regularized to guarantee an active market, a flow of assets and healthy supply/demand balance.

Foreign exchange market is not centralized and does not have a fixed oversight regulation; therefore, it is an over the counter market. The main challenge with over the counter markets is that the trader will have to conduct a due diligence investigation to confirm the reputation and trading practices of the brokers before opening an account with them. Again, lighter regulatory protection might put the trader at risk because; depending on the country that one is trading in, he/she may have no way of getting compensated if he/she feels that the broker gave unfair treatment.

Fewer residual returns

Some trade instruments such as bonds and stocks have a regular schedule for payment of dividends and interests; therefore, they have an enhanced long-term value. However, foreign exchange trade aims at gaining immediate capital gains from a currency pair when one currency appreciates. Again, the forex exchange can either get or pay interest when a position is held overnight. This varies depending on the country that is issuing the currency.

Summary of the pros and cons of the forex market

To a large extent, the foreign exchange market is accessible, potentially lucrative and flexible. The trading environment is extensive (all over the world), liquid and transparent therefore good for traders. When one takes into account the inherent risks of the trade, he will find that most of them are present in all other markets and trading activities. As such the forex market offers ample opportunities for a trader to succeed if he/she is willing to come to terms with the inherent characteristics and conventions of the currency market.

Chapter 2: Opening a Brokerage Account

Basically, foreign exchange involves buying and selling of different currencies across the world. The number of participants in this market is very large; therefore, the liquidity is very high. The most unique aspect of the forex trade is that individual traders can compete against large institutions such as banks and hedge funds; all one needs to do is to select the right account and set it up.

There are different types of accounts, but the traders have three main options namely mini accounts, standard accounts, and managed accounts. Each account has its own advantages and disadvantages. The type of account that one opts for depends on factors such as the size of initial capital, risk tolerance levels, and the hours one has to analyze the charts either daily or at different intervals.

Mini Trading Accounts

Simply put, a mini account is one that allows the trader to transact using mini lots. For most brokerage firms, one mini lot equals to 10,000 units. That is equal to 1/10 of a standard account. Brokerage firms offer mini lots in order to attract new traders who are still hesitant to trade with bigger accounts or those who do not have the investment funds required.

The advantages of Mini accounts include low risk, low capital required and flexibility. The trader can trade in increments of 10,000 units; therefore, if he/she is inexperienced, he/she does not have to worry about blowing through their account and capital. Experienced traders can use mini accounts to test new strategies without excessive risk. A mini account can be opened with as little as $100, $250 or $500 and the leverage can go up to 400:1. A risk management plan is the key to successful trading and in the case of selecting lots; a trader can minimize the risk by buying a number of mini lots to minimize risk. Remember that one standard lot is equal to about 10 mini lots and diversification reduces risk.

The main disadvantage of mini accounts is a low reward. The lower the risk, the lower the reward. A mini lot account can only produce $1 per pip movement if it is trading 10000 lots. In a standard account, one pip movement equals to $10.

A subset of the mini account is the micro account which is offered by some online broker. This account has very little risk and also very little reward. The trade is 1000 base currency units, and one pip movement earns or loses 10 cents. These accounts are best suited for traders who have very little knowledge about forex trade, and one can open using as little as 25 dollars.

Standard Trading Accounts

The standard trading accounts are the most common for traders especially the experienced ones. These accounts give trader access to lots of currency worth 100,000 units each. This, however, does not mean that a trader has to put $100,000 in the account as capital so as to trade. The rules of leverage and margin mean that all a trader need is $1000 to have a margin account.

The main advantage of this account is the large reward that one might reap with the right strategy and predictions. One pip movement earns $ 10. Again, individuals who own such accounts get better services and perks because of the upfront capital investment in the account.

The disadvantages include high initial capital and potential for loss. The kind of capital required to set up a standard account can deter many traders from venturing in it. Again, the higher the risk, the higher the returns and the vice versa holds, A standard account trader has a higher risk of loss because if a lot falls with 100 pips, he/she loses $1000. Such can be devastating for beginner traders.

Managed Trading Accounts

Managed accounts are accounts where one puts in the capital but does not make the decisions to sell or buy. Such accounts are handled by account managers such as stockbrokers and stock managers. In this case, the traders set objectives for the managers (the expected returns, risk management) and the managers have to meet them.

Managed accounts are categorized into two major types namely Pooled funds and Individual accounts. In pooled funds, the money of different investors is put into an investment vehicle referred to as mutual fund and the profits generated are shared. The accounts are further classified by risk tolerance. If a trader is looking for higher returns, he/she may put his money in a high risk/reward account while those looking for long term steady income can invest in lower risk accounts. Under managed accounts, the individual accounts are managed by a broker each in its own capacity, unlike the pooled funds where the manager uses all the money together.

The main advantage of managed accounts is that one gets professional advice and guidance. An experienced professional forex account manager will be making the decisions, and this is a benefit that one can use. Again, a trader gets to trade without having to spend hours analyzing the charts and watching for developments.

One disadvantage that deters traders from venturing into this account is the high price. One should be aware that the majority of managed accounts require one to put in at least $2000 in the pooled account and $10000 for the individual accounts. To add to this cost, the managers are entitled to a commission which is calculated monthly or yearly. The managed accounts are also very inflexible for the trader. If he/she sees an opportunity to trade, he/she will not be able to make a move but will rely on the manager to decide.

Note

It is advisable for a trader to use the demo accounts offered by brokers before investing in real money regardless of the account he/she opts to use. Demo accounts allow one to practice without risk and also to try out different strategies. One rule that every trader should apply is to never invest in a real account unless they are completely satisfied with it. One of the main differences between success and failure in forex exchange is the account selected.

Opening an Account

Forex exchange has been around for very many years, and some say that it is as old as the invention of national currencies. Over the years, the market has grown so much so that it is the biggest market across the world. However, it has not been accessible to the public as easily as it is today. From the 1990s when the era of the internet begun, many retail forex brokers have established routes through which anyone can trade in currencies so long as they can access the internet and have some money. There is a lot of hype and information about forex trade on the internet, but not everybody understands how to select and open an account.

Currently, opening a forex account has become as easy as opening a bank account or another type of brokerage account. Some of the typical requirements are a name, phone number, address, email, a password, account currency type, country of citizenship, date of birth, employment status, and tax ID or Social security number. Opening an account may also require one to answer some financial questions such as their net worth, annual income, trading objectives, and trading experience. Before one starts to trade on the foreign exchange market, they should make some considerations to ensure that they have a positive, secure and successful experience.

The right broker

The first step to trading well is to find the right broker. The activities of forex exchange are decentralized, and there are hardly any regulations. Because of the over the counter nature, traders are advised to identify a reliable broker. This involves conducting researches on the reputation of the broker; to identify if there is a history of irregular practices. One may also want to comprehensively understand the services offered by the particular broker before setting up an account. While some brokerages support basic and plain vanilla activities, others offer very sophisticated trading platforms. Some brokers will offer the trader analytical resources to support better decision making while others won't.

Again, a trader should assess the fees and commissions for different brokers. The majority of Brokers charge some fees for their services through the bid-ask spread and, in many cases, it is not a large percentage. However, some brokerages have some other fees and commissions, and they might be hidden from the trader. When one is considering the extra costs, he/she should check if it is worthwhile.

The procedure

Opening a foreign exchange account is not hard, but traders should have a few things in order to get started. The trader will have to provide some identification information such as name, phone number, country of origin et cetera. Besides, the trader will be required to state his/her trade intentions and their level of knowledge and experience in the trade. The steps of opening an account may vary depending on the brokerage firm, but normally it involves:

- Accessing the website of the broker and study the accounts available. The accounts include small ones where the trader can trade with minimum capital such as mini accounts or the sophisticated accounts designed for experienced traders such as standard trading account.
- Completing an application form,
- Getting registered (user name and password) in order to access the account.
- Log in to the client portal and arrange for a transfer of money from the bank to the forex account. These deposits can be made through credit or debit card, checks, or electronic transfers.
- Once the funds are transferred, the trader is ready to start trading. Before trading, the trader may review the recommendations made by the brokers or extra services offered such as simulator programs.

The use of margins

Once a trader has opened an account, he/she has to decide whether to apply a margin or not. A margin is a leverage move whereby the broker offers the trader a loan in order to increase the available capital. A broker can offer a margin on capital for any rate between 50:1 and 400:1 depending on the country they operate from. The amount that a trader wants in terms of margin will determine the amount of capital that he/she will deposit in the account. The deposit acts as collateral for the trading activities. True, margins increase potential profits, but one should be warned that they also increase the risks. In case of loss, the trader will be required to cover the costs even if they are beyond the initial investment.

Chapter 3:
Currency Pairs and PIPS

Prices are always in terms of the price of one currency relative to another. Learning how to read and understand quoted data is important, and you need to have a thorough understanding of what everything is referring to. The good thing is that this is not really very complicated, so most readers will pick it up in a short amount of time. In addition to learning about currency pairs, we will need to learn how prices are quotes and the all-important "pips" that you may have heard about when people discuss Forex. We will get started by looking at currency pairs first.

Currency Pair Trading

When you are trading currency, you are trading one currency against another. So, what does this mean? Essentially, you buy one currency and sell the other simultaneously.

You need to understand how you would buy or sell currency pairs based on the market conditions that you are anticipating. Let's use the Euro and US Dollar currency pair as an example.

If you believe that the Euro will strengthen against the US Dollar, then you would buy the EUR/USD currency pair, which means you are buying Euros and selling dollars. Conversely, if you believe that the Dollar is going to strengthen against the Euro, or put another way that the Euro will weaken against the dollar, then you would sell the EUR/USD currency pair. In that case, it means that you are selling Euros and buying dollars.

Currencies are priced relative to one another, and they are always quoted in pairs. For example, the Euro and the US Dollar are one of the currency pairs. Currency pairs are ordered, and the ordering is always the same. For the Euro and the US Dollar, it will appear like this:

EUR/USD

The currency on the left side is the primary, or base currency.

The currency on the right side is the secondary. The order never changes, this is just the standard, and it's for trading and ordering purposes only. So you will not see USD/EUR quoted. It does not have anything to do with one currency value versus another or anything of the sort. The ordering of the pairs has the practical significance that we described above. So if you want to buy Euros because you think that the Euro is going to go up with respect to the dollar, then you buy EUR/USD. Or consider the pair GBP/AUD, which pairs the Great British Pound and the Australian Dollar. If you think that the Great British pound is going to go up against the Australian Dollar, then you would buy the currency pair. That means you are buying Great British Pounds and selling Australian Dollars. On the other hand, if you believe that the Great British Pound is going to go down with respect to the Australian Dollar, then you would sell the currency pair, meaning that you're selling Great British Pounds and buying Australian dollars.

Many of these currencies are referred to by nicknames that are of historical origin. It's good to know what these nicknames are in case you get involved with conversations about currency trading, as experienced traders may throw around this terminology. You would not want to be lost in a conversation because you didn't know what the nicknames are. You may also on occasion see the nicknames used in articles and such.

Some of the nicknames are obvious. The Australian dollar is often referred to in shorthand form as the Aussie. The US Dollar is known as the greenback. This name will not surprise anyone. The New Zealand dollar sometimes goes by the name Kiwi.

A couple of more obscure names exist as well. The Great British Pound, while sometimes known by the name pound sterling, also gets referred to by some as the cable. The origin of its term is moderately interesting. In the days when electronic communications networks were first being established, the name cable came about because trading was done by undersea cables between the U.S. and Great Britain, and so American bankers began referring to the Pound as the cable. Somehow this name has stuck through more than 100 years of usage.

Another interesting name is for the Canadian dollar, which sometimes gets referred to as the Loonie. This comes from the name of the dollar coin that the country used to have with a duck on one side of the coin.

The Majors

The currencies of the main developed countries and the European Union are known as the "majors." These include the US Dollar, the Euro, the Japanese Yen, the Swiss Franc, the Australian dollar, the New Zealand dollar, the Canadian dollar, and the Great British Pound. The symbols used for these are USD, EUR, JPY, CHF, AUD, NZD, CAD, and GBP, respectively.

But when someone says the "majors" they are really talking about the currency pairs that these are involved in. The major currency pairs include:

- *EUR/USD*
- *USD/JPY*
- *GBP/USD*
- *USD/CAD*
- *USD/CHF*
- *AUD/USD*
- *NZD/USD*

The majors make up the vast majority of the trading on the Forex markets. But as you might imagine, there are many different currency pairs. In fact, they can number 100 currency pairs. There can be money to made trading currencies that are not majors. You have to be careful when looking at other currency pairs because you might find yourself in a liquidity trap.

You know from finance that liquidity is a measure of how quickly you can convert an asset into cash. Something that is readily converted into cash is highly liquid. Therefore, a gold bar is pretty liquid, you can run down to a precious metals store and sell it for cash right away. A house is less liquid. While it can be converted into cash, it might take some time to sell it. When the markets are hot, it might sell in a few days or weeks, but it could take months at other times. If you needed money to pay for a car repair, selling your house would not be a good strategy, but selling a gold bar would allow you to raise the money nearly immediately.

In the currency markets, liquidity means you can either buy back a currency pair (if you sold it to open your position) or you can sell it (if you bought it to open) quickly. As we will see, when you are watching currency pairs on the charts, the time frame over, which you may need to make a move to close your position, can be very small. So it's important to be able to move quickly.

Many people, including some experts that you might run into on the internet, might be promoting the idea that you can make money trading minor currencies, like the Mexican Peso. There is a lot of software out there that will find currency pairs that are trending for you. That is all well and good, except it's not so good if you are trying to enter a trade when you identify it forming, and it takes so long that by the time your order is filled, it's nearing the peak in a price increase. Alternatively, you might be following a trend, and it starts showing signs that the trend is coming to a reversal. That is the time to get out of the trade. But you might get in a situation where you can't close your position quickly because it's a currency pair with low liquidity.

For that reason, you might want to stay away from minor currencies. The action is in the majors, and one thing about the majors is you won't have to worry about the kinds of problems that I have just described. Liquidity also impacts the cost of trading. The less liquid a currency pair is, the higher the cost of trading it.

There are currency pairs that involve some of the currencies from developed countries, which do have relatively high trading volume. These are composed of the major currencies when they are paired with each other but not with the US dollar. These include:

- GBP/CHF: Great British Pound and Swiss Franc.
- GBP/CAD: Great British Pound and Canadian Dollar.
- GBP/AUD: Great British Pound and Australian Dollar.
- GBP/JPY: Great British Pound and Japanese Yen.
- EUR/GBP: Euro and Great British Pound.
- EUR/AUD: Euro and Australian Dollar
- EUR/NZD: Euro and New Zealand Dollar
- EUR/JPY: Euro and Japanese Yen
- EUR/CHF: Euro and Swiss Franc
- EUR/CAD: Euro and Canadian Dollar
- CHF/JPY: Swiss Franc, and Japanese Yen
- AUD/JPY: Australian Dollar and Japanese Yen
- NZD/JPY: New Zealand Dollar and Japanese Yen
- CAD/JPY: Canadian Dollar and Japanese Yen

Next, we come to the so-called "exotics." These are currency pairs between a major and a strong economy that isn't considered one of the majors. So the USD or Euro can be paired with each of these currencies. Some of the "exotics" include Sweden, Norway, Singapore, Hong Kong, Denmark, South Africa, and Turkey. The exotics are not traded as much and so can be considered to be illiquid. As a beginning trader, they are probably best avoided. Some currency pairs that you will see include the Mexican Peso (MXN) and the Chinese currency (sometimes called the Yuan) CNH.

It doesn't end there, of course; you can trade currencies for nearly every country on earth that has one, so, for example, you could trade the Mexican Peso in one of its currency pairs. However, these currency pairs may be illiquid as well. As long as you can get in and out of the trade quickly, it's considered to be a good currency pair.

Summary: How Currency Pairs Work

Let's set up a hypothetical or generic currency pair to review the basic concepts.

(currency one) / (currency two)

When you say you are buying the currency pair, that means you are buying currency one and selling currency two. You will do this if you believe that currency one will rise in value with respect to currency two.

Or put another way, you believe that currency two is going to drop in value, relative to currency one. The currency pair is always quoted in this manner.

If you believe that currency two is going to rise in value with respect to currency one, then you would sell the currency pair. This is a bet that currency one is going to decline in value relative to currency two.

If the currency pair in question was EUR/CAD, buying the pair means you are betting on the Euro, and selling the pair means you are betting on the CAD.

It might sound a little bit like we are beating a dead horse, but this concept is important. Let's think about how this is going to work out in a chart. The Forex market will let you look at charts of currency pairs, and they look a lot like stock market charts. But it's important to understand the direction of the curve since we are talking about pairs.

If we have a chart for A/B, then if the curve is going up, that indicates an increasing price for the currency pair A/B. And what that means is that currency A is increasing in value, while currency B is decreasing in value. If you had bought the currency pair A/B, then this would be a winning trade for you.

On the other hand, if the curve was going downward, this would be favorable for currency B – indicating that it was going up while currency A was going down in value.

Remember that everything is relative when it comes to currency trading, there are not absolutes. So, it's all about the price of once currency relative to another. That may or may not impact other currency pairs.

Here is an example: the chart below is for the AUD/USD currency pair. On the left-hand side, the price is decreasing, by a lot, but on the right-hand side, it made a steep climb upwards. Using what we just learned, you realize that on the left side of the chart, the value of the Australian Dollar was decreasing relative to the US Dollar, or you could put it in terms of saying the US dollar is increasing relative to the Australian Dollar. So on the left-hand side of the chart, if you had bought the currency pair, you probably would not have been too happy at that point. But if you had sold the currency pair – and therefore favored the US Dollar, for that time frame your bet was favored.

Meanwhile on the right side of the chart, as the curve is moving upward, if you had bought the currency pair, you'd be happy because an upward trend of the pair means that it was increasing in value – the Australian dollar was rising against the US Dollar. If you had sold the pair, well, in this case, you were losing money.

The price of the pair is listed on the right-hand side. This means one Australian dollar is worth $0.69 in US dollars. You can invert that (1/0.69) to express how many Australian dollars a US dollar would buy; the answer is 1.45.

PIPS

If you get into Forex trading, the concept of a pip is one of the most important that you will come across. Essentially, a pip is a measure of a price change in a currency pair, and it can be considered to be the most significant measure to make. Small pips mean big money when you are trading lots of currency. So it is crucial to understand a pip. We might begin by asking what does this phrase mean. It is nothing more than an acronym, and you must familiarize yourself with what it stands for.

PIP Means *percentage in point*. It can also mean the price interest point, but most people think of it in terms of percentage in point. In truth, most traders probably don't think about the formal definition, but they know how to work with pips and what the meaning is, when looking at prices of currency pairs.

To understand how to use pips on a practical level, you must look at how currency pair prices are quoted. Most currency pairs are actually quoted to five decimal places. It used to be four decimal places, but this has changed in recent years. One pip is a one-point change in the fourth decimal place. Let's suppose that the EUR/USD pair is quoted as: 1.14671

This is not real value; I have made this up for illustration purposes. The number to note is number 7, which lies in the fourth decimal place. This is the pip. If this value were to change to: 1.14681

Then there has a been a 1 pip move for the EUR/USD currency pair. We can practice some more. If the price moves to: 1.14781

It has changed in price by 0.00100. That is, the price went up by 10 pips. Now suppose that it changes to: 1.14731

If you take the difference, you get 0.00050 – that is, the price has dropped by five pips.

You are already becoming an expert at Forex trading. But you will notice that we have added a fifth number. The firth number is called the "pipette." Sometimes, the pipette is shown in a smaller font. Generally speaking, the pipette is not all that important. You can do well in Forex trading without worrying about pipettes. It is such a small number that it hardly matters for anything, but at least you know that it is there and what it is called. So if someone calls you and says that the GBP/JPY pair moved by 1 pipette, you know that the 5th decimal place has increased in value by one. But does it mean anything to the trader, as far as gaining or losing money? Not really.

Japanese Yen

When learning about pips, there is a special case of the Japanese Yen. In this case, pips are treated differently than they are for every other currency. The reason that this is so is quite simple. This has to do with the value or scale of the Japanese Yen as compared to other currencies. The Japanese Yen is a smaller currency than others that are traded. You might think of this by imagining that instead of the US Dollar, the 25-cent coin was the standard measure of US currency. That is all it is, and it's no more complicated than that; the Japanese Yen is just denominated at a smaller level.

It is quite a popular currency. So, it pays to know where the pip is for the Japanese Yen, since it is quite a bit different from the pips of the other currencies. The special rule here is this. For the Japanese yen, the 2d decimal place is the pip. The third decimal place is the pipette. So, if you see a quote for Japanese Yen that was, say: 110.873

The pip, in this case, is the number in the second decimal place, which would be 7. The pipette is the number that is found in the third decimal place. So, in this example, it is 3. Now suppose that our price quote undergoes the following transformation: 110.893

This means that the price has risen by 2 pips. If it now goes to: 110.894

That means it has risen by one pipette. Now suppose there is a further change in the value. This time it goes to: 110.853

This time, it has dropped four pips, and also by one pipette. Do you see how simple this is? To be truthful, Forex trading is so simple that a child who has not yet entered high school can grasp the basic facts of Forex trading. Show this to your children, and they will learn all about pips and pipettes.

How Traders Talk About Pips

You are going to hear different conversations about pips when you are following the Forex markets. Included in this discussion is going to be some talk about how the price of a currency pair has changed. Right now, I am looking at the USD/RUR currency pair. RUR is the Russian Ruble. In this case, the value is: 63.54494

What is the pip? Try and figure it out before I give you the answer. This will test whether or not you are gaining knowledge. You can stop reading here if you need to.

Remember that for any currency pair other than the Japanese Yen, the pip is the fourth decimal place. Therefore, the pip is 9 in this case.

What if a trader told you that the US/RUR currency pair moved 50 pips? What on earth does this mean? It simply means that we add 50 pips to the value above. This is done by adding to the fourth decimal place, but it's the third since it's a power of ten.

Moved by 50 pips -> 63.54494 +0.00500 = 63.54994

Of course, I am saying that it went up by 50 pips. This might be a bit of assumption; it could have gone down 50 pips, the trader used the word "moved." Without further information, this could be the assumption to make. But you may ask to get clarification, if you are not completely sure of the direction of movement. If it went down 60 pips instead, then we would see a price movement in the following manner:

Down 60 pips -> 63.54494 - 0.00600 = 63.53894

And what is the pipette in this case? It is the number in the fifth decimal place, which is 4.

Price Quotes, Spread, Buying, and Selling

When you bring up price quotes for a currency pair, you are going to see them in two columns. Here is a real-time list of quotes from meta trader 5 that I have pulled up while writing this book:

EURUSD	1.11399	1.11404
GBPUSD	1.21823	1.21832
USDCHF	0.99137	0.99146
USDJPY	108.775	108.782
USDCNH	6.88852	6.88988
USDRUB	63.54402	63.55333
AUDUSD	0.69054	0.69061
NZDUSD	0.66299	0.66311
USDCAD	1.31665	1.31671
USDSEK	9.48899	9.49212
EURRUB	70.726	70.749
USDRUR	63.54494	63.55455
USDHKD	7.82281	7.82290

For a new trader, this can be a bit confusing. We will now explore what these numbers mean. If you are trading Forex, these are the types of price quotes that you are going to see on your trading platform. Therefore, it is important to know what they mean so that you are not in for any surprises when you trade a currency pair. Let us look at the top number, which is the famous EUR/USD currency pair, that makes up something like 35% of all currency trades on most days.

On the left-hand side, we see 1.11399. But on the right-hand side, we see 1.11404. What are these two numbers? It turns out that the number that is shown as the price on the left-hand side of a currency pair quote is the selling price. So, in this example, 1.11399 is the selling price for the EUR/USD currency pair. The other price, which is found in the column on the right-hand side, is the buying price. The buying price is always going to be higher than the selling price!

This difference in price is called the spread. So, to compute the spread, enter the value on the right-hand side into your spreadsheet or calculator. Then subtract the value on the left-hand side. That will tell you what the spread is for each currency pair.

For the Euro and US Dollar pair, we have the following spread:

1.11404 − 1.11399 = 0.00500

The 5 is in the third decimal place. The pip is the fourth decimal place. So, it's a power of ten higher. That means the spread, in this case, is 50 pips. So, it costs 50 pips more to buy the EUR/USD pair than it does to sell it. If you were to sell the pair, you'd receive the price 1.11399, while if you were to buy the pair, you'd have to put up 1.11404. Now, does that sound fair? Well, the Forex dealer has to make their money in one way or another, and this is the method used for charging commissions.

Let us choose another example. These are the price quotes from the USD/HKD pair that you can see in the figure. The quoted value in the left-hand column is the selling price.

ON the left side, we have 7.82281 for the USD/HKD pair. That means if you want to sell the USD/HKD pair, this is the price you will sell it for. On the right side, we see 7.82290. The fourth decimal place is the pip, so there is a 1 pip spread between these prices.

So, what is a spread exactly? Our past conversations on this should give a pretty clear hint. A spread is a markup price put there by the FX Dealer. I said it was a commission, but that is not really the case. When it comes to Forex trading, brokers actually make money from two things. They make money from the spread, that much is sure. But some brokers will offer tighter spreads. But brokers or Forex dealers, whatever you want to call them, are definitely not charities. They have to make money to stay in operation, and the fact is if they are giving you a smaller spread, they have to make up the money in some other way. This is done by charging a commission. This means that a Forex dealer or broker is going to make money from spreads and commissions.

Buying and Selling

The spread is something that is important to pay attention to. First lets us say what will happen if you enter a trade by various methods. Well, actually there are only two ways that you can enter the Forex trade. The first method that can be used is buying the currency pair. If you buy the currency pair, then you are going to start the trade-up by a small amount, because the buy quote on the right-hand side is always a little bit higher than the sell quote on the left side.

So if the currency pair was the AUD/USD from the image above, the price quotes are listed here as: 0.69054 0.69061

We should immediately quote this in pips. There is a 1 pip difference here. The left side of this number pair, 0.69054, is the selling price. That is a bet that AUD/USD is going to drop in value. Or put another way, it's a bet that the Australian Dollar is going to drop with respect to the US Dollar. It can even be put in a third way still. That third way to say it is that you are betting that the US dollar is going to rise in value, as compared to the Australian dollar.

The left-hand number is the SELL price for the trade. So we could sell for 0.69054, which also means that we would be selling Australian dollars and simultaneously buying US Dollars.

The spread is important because if you sell to open a new position on the Forex market, that means we have to buy it back to close the trade. That is a little bit weird for new traders to wrap their heads around because most of us are used to the conventional way to use the stock market. That is, we buy stocks at a low price, and then we sell those stocks at a higher market price when the time is right.

You can loosely think of a trade when you sell to open a currency pair as shorting the currency pair. We are hoping that it will drop in value because then when we buy it back, it will be cheaper and we make a profit on the difference. So this is very much like shorting the stock.

But if you will notice since the value quoted on the right-hand side, which is the buy price for the currency pair, is always higher than the price given for selling, that means you always open selling prices down by a given number of pips. That doesn't matter, typically the number of pips that you open down is going to be a small number. The values of these currency pairs can move by large amounts over the course of just one trading day. Just in the few minutes that I have been writing this passage, the prices quoted have changed. For the EUR/USD currency pair, you can remember that we started out with this: 1.11399 1.11404

Now it's already changed to this: 1.11415 1.11420

The selling price, which would be the price on the left-hand side here, has risen by 1 pip and 6 pipettes. On the other side, the buying side, its risen by 2 pips. The spread has, in fact, narrowed a bit.

If you buy a currency pair, obviously you have to sell it back in order to close a trade. So buying a currency pair is more along the lines of conventional thinking, that is it will be like the buy low, sell high mentality.

You have to wrap your mind around both modes of thinking, however. You are simply not going to want to be buying currency pairs all the time, because circumstances are always changing. So while one day it might be advantageous to buy a currency pair, a few days later it might be far better to sell a currency pair. Therefore, it will become important to understand the concept of selling to open a trade, and then buying it back to close the trade.

But in currency exchanges, it is really not all that mysterious. If you sell to open the USD/RUR currency pair, that means you are selling US Dollars to buy Russian Rubles. If you buy to open the currency pair, then you are buying US Dollars and selling Russian Rubles.

It really is that simple, and when you sell to open you star the trade down a bit.

Some brokers will offer a rebate. This means that some of the spread will be paid back to the trader. Please check with your individual broker for details.

SWAPS

Another concept that you have to become familiar with when it comes to Forex trading involves what are called swaps. A swap is involved with the payment of interest rates. When you hold currency, that means that you can earn interest on the currency. Well, to be honest, it depends on the situation. You need to know the interest rates in each country of the currency pair in order to determine whether or not you will earn interest. Consider the following currency pair, for the sake of our discussion here: GBP/CAD

This currency pair is the Great British Pound and the Canadian Dollar. Now for the sake of argument, say that you have bought the currency pair. If you have a higher interest rate for Great Britain, as compared to Canada, that would mean that you would earn interest overnight. For the sake of example if the interest rate in Great Britain was 3%, but it was 2% in Canada, that means that if you old the currency pair overnight, you will earn 1% interest.

But you can pay interest on currency pairs held overnight as well. If the interest rates were switched, that is if the interest rate in Great Britain was 2% and the interest rate in Canada was 3% - and we bought the currency pair, then that would mean that if we held it overnight, we would have to pay interest.

If you sell the currency pair, then the opposite situation holds. If Great Britain has a higher interest rate than Canada, and you sell the currency pair GBP/CAD, and you keep your position overnight, then you would owe interest. On the other hand, if Great Britain had a lower interest rate than Canada, and you had sold the currency pair, then you would earn interest overnight.

This might sound like important talk, but the reality is that it's not going to be that important for most Forex traders. And that is probably going to include yourself. The reality is that the amounts of interest that we are talking about here tend to be very small. This is true generally speaking and to be quite honest about this; it's even truer now. The reason is that most central banks throughout the world are charging low-interest rates. So the only time this is going to be important is if you are making large trades, and you hold the position for a long time period. If you hold the position for a long time, then each night that rolls over there will be a new calculation of interest either paid or received. So on one time, it might be small, but small things can add up. Therefore, if you hold your position for 120 days, then it will add up 120 times, and this could possibly make a difference. But even then, it's going to be a small amount of money, relatively speaking. I will say that in today's environment of small interest rates, and small differences in interest rates between the major central banks, that nobody is going to get rich trying to earn interest in this fashion.

Chapter 4: Fundamental and Technical Analysis

As a trader, you can be confused about whether to opt for a technical or analysis, but it doesn't matter. As long as you learn the best time to enter or exit a trade, you can choose one or a combination of these analyses. But, before choosing any, you need to understand how both work and if they will assist you in making good trading decisions.

Fundamental analysis requires economic and statistical data too. Also, it uses data to determine currency strength. On the other hand, technical analysis use chat patterns to forecast price movements. Like flags and triangles.

Well, read on to get insights on the similarities and differences between fundamental and technical analysis.

What is the fundamental analysis?

Fundamental analysis looks at the market an interesting perspective. It analyses social, political, and economic factors that may affect the demand and supply of an asset. Fundamental analysis strives to find out the actual value of an asset, give a comparison to the current price, and also locate a trading opportunity. In the Forex world, supply and demand determine the currency exchange rate. Also, it aims to look at different factors which determine the country's economy is doing well or is facing an economic crisis. Lastly, it analyses the financial market with the aim of predicting future prices.

Price of an asset can differ from time to time sometimes the markets may underprice, misprice, or overprice an asset. But, later, the market often normalizes price. These are fundamental analysis.

A stable economy strengthens the country's currency and vice versa. To obtain a country currency, then one has to purchase its asset. Well, foreign investors, business people usually invest in a country to get access to their currency.

When a country economy improves, then, their dollar is most likely to gain strength. Fundamental analysis often tends to predict a projection on business performance. Investors use a broader spectrum of the stock market to evaluate the review of economic factors like its strength and specific market conditions.

Also, it evaluates show to manage and make business decisions and also determine credit risk. Valuate a stock and predict when the price will evolve.

Factors that are affect countries economics

Several factors contribute to the decline or incline of a country's economy. They include:
- *Unemployment rates*
- *Monetary policy*
- *Housing stats*
- *International trade a*
- *Manufacturing*

Fundamental factors that influence currency movement

Economic indicators

An economic indicator is a piece of detailed information about the country financial status. It's released by the government or an organization. The results are released at particular scheduled times that are: weekly, monthly, or even quarterly.

The information released can lead to higher returns in the financial markets. With the data, one can determine whether a countries economy has improved, is stagnant or has decreased. The commotion can occur when prices are released before the release of official rates. This condition is known as "priced market."

When reports are released, traders usually check on the weakness and strength in the various economies before venturing into a trade. The following are economic indicators you should watch out.

Interest rates

Interest rates have an impact on the unemployment rate, investment trade production, and inflation. There is a different kind of interest rates; central banks around the world usually offer loan to banks, business, and citizens of a country. Sometimes the central bank can decide to lower the interest's rates so to stabilize an economy.

But, when the interest's rates are too low, and lots of loans are issued, then it's likely to taint lousy image on the economy. That's why they sometimes regulate by raising it.

Interest rates are an excellent place to look for trading opportunities. They tend to control economies growth. High-interest rates make financial assets attractive, thus luring more investors to invest, and the result, is the currency value increases.

Inflation

Inflation is the prices of goods in a period over time. The government and the central banks work to enhance the balance. When the inflations rates are high, then the value of the currency is likely to depreciate

Most developed countries believe that moderate inflation signifies a growing economy in developed nations. On the other hand, developing nations believe that a decreased or maintain inflation is excellent as it keeps the country economy check.

Gross domestic products (GDP)

GDP contains a total market of value of goods and services produced in the country yearly. GDP Increases in an unhealthy for the particular nation.

Industrial production

Usually, shows the productivity of factories, mines industries, and utilities in a nation. Traders who use the utility industry before deciding to trade can be significantly affected by the changes in weather. Weather sometimes causes volatility to the currency of a particular nation.

When you chose fundamental analysis, you should consider the following factors to maximize your results.

- Have an economic calendar- in your calendar; you can list indicators as well as look into the future market.

- Check what's trending on the economic market- you should keep up with the information the economic news and watch out the news that could be a threat to your trade and vice versa.
- Give it time- don't react immediately to the news released. Take your time as rush decisions may hurt your trade. Numbers usually get changed, and sometimes they are revised. The more patient you are, the more good choices you are likely to make.
- Understand the market expectations of particular data. Check if the expectations of a requirement are met. The information is more useful than the data provided.

Tools for fundamental analysis

You need to understand the depths of fundamentals analysis. The knowledge of the key ratios will help you follow stocks more accurately and carefully. Most fundamental tools focus on growth, earning, and the value that is in the market.

Price to earnings ratio (P/E) - this ratio shows a comparison of current sales of a market stock and their share per earnings.

Earnings per share (EPS) - investigates what percentages of profit the company stock assigns

Dividend yield- usually expressed as a percentage. Paid in a yearly period and lastly, it compares to the annual shared price.

Price to sale ratio (P/R-) compares company stalk to the revenues.

Projected earnings growth (PEG)- analyses a year's growth of a stock

Price to book ratio (P/B) – also known as the price to equity ratio. You can determine this ratio when determine by diving a closing the stock most present closing price and the value of the last quarter of the book to the cost per share.

The price to book ratio - the price to book ratio shows asset value as it appears in the company books.

Return on equity- to get a return on equity; you divide shareholder equity with the company's net income.

Advantages of fundamental analysis

Uses analytical data- the results ensure that there is no bias. The results found are sound financial data making it concrete to use.

Easy to understand- the accounting financial analysis will help you understand better how the market works

There is a focus- fundamental analysis not only focus one, but several long-term elements like demographics, economics, technology, and consumer trends to get the desired results.

Use a systematic approaching to get values- the analytical and statistical tools you use enables you to choose whether to buy or sell in a trade.

Disadvantages

Takes a lot of time- to get accurate results, you have to dig into various economic indicators. Usually, it not only takes time but you need to be willing to work hard and obtain the results that you need.

Lots of assumptions involved- there is a lot of assumptions involved in forecasting financials, you should expect the best, and the worst scenarios as unexpected politic and economic change can result in problems.

Technical analysis

Technical analysis is a theoretical framework used by Forex traders to study price movement. A trader can consider a historical price movement. You study the price pattern of a particular specific asset. Additionally, you use indicators, technical studies, and other analysis tools before embarking on a trade. You should check what happens and make a potential price movement. Charts are easy to visualize; you can see clearly how the market is fairing on. Additionally, you can view past data, current trends, and predicts what the future would be like.

Chart watching basics you should know;

Moving averages

Helps tin determine the overall trading. A trend condition usually, it plots the average price of a security in a particular period.

Price trends

Checks I stock price are accelerating or decelerating. And the amount of time and the period in which the price has stayed his way. Most chartists buy a security that is up in the trends.

Volume

Volume acts as lie detectors. With volume, one can predict how strong a trend influence may be. Decreasing volume indicates that a trend can be on the verge of a reversal.

Appear above or below a chart.

All the information on a current market is reflected on a price. When you know the history of the trading market, you will be able to make great trading decisions. It acts as a map, guiding you on how to curate or conduct a trade.

Technical analysis was self-fulfilling as it's subjective. Technicians use various methods to study the price patterns. That is;

Technical analysis candle- candle patterns show high, low, open, and close levels. With this, you can get clues on how the buyers and sellers reacted during the previous years.

Technical analysis chart - the chart gives clarity to buyers and sellers throughout the market.

Technical analysis indicators- using this chart as trade will help you understand the market conditions. You will also view the rising and the falling momentums of the market

Importance of a Technical Analysis

There are many uncertainties in this market. But as a trader, you have to take a risk and work on probabilities. As much as the market can be chaotic, you will identify patterns and make the most out of it. With a clear review of the charts, and study of the market, you have the potential of making the correct choices when it comes to your trade. You will know when to enter a market. And, the most important thing is, you learn how to get out of a trade and when.

Secondly, you learn to identify patterns mark can figure out what to do when particular issues arise in the market.

Also, you get to learn to determine the probabilities and jump into the right opportunities, when odds work on your favor.

How do you conduct a technical analysis?

Determine which security interests you -For instance, you can do research on which sector is at the moment trading this will assist in deciding on what to buy or sell

Choose a strategy that suits you -each stock is unique. And each cannot utilize the same approach.

Choose a trading account. To maximize profits, go for the account with the right functionality, cost, and also support.

Comprehend your tools -Knowing thee tools that fit your trading strategies and tools is essential. Free tools are available for you to learn and understand the features.

Try out to test your system with the market data before jumping on the bandwagon of trading. Choose a few indicators that can fit the technical indicator requirements you chose. Monitor how they perform each day.

Advantages of technical analysis

You learn when to exist and enter a trade- through the patterns in charts; you will learn how to jump out of a trade.

They provide you with the right information directions are essential to in any field. Technical analysis offers precisely what you need to navigate this industry.

*Get information on the current tren*ds- prices tend to increase or decrease. Usually, they reflect on the information of an existing asset to make decisions.

Differences between fundamental and technical analysis

As much as the two analysis help you get trading results. They have numerous differences. Some are here below

1. Fundamental analysis uses economic m reports of industry statistics and news events to analyze data and make predictions; also, it forecasts share prices on the basis company statics and economic industry. Technical analysis uses a chart to analyze data and majorly focuses on internal data and market statistics.
2. Fundamental analysis is concerned with the investments. The investors usually hold or buy a stock of a company with the information got. Technical analysis is more concerned with the trade.

3. The security of the future prices us determine by the past and present performance a company make in Forex trading, while indicators and charts are the ones that determine the future market prices
4. A long-term trader usually utilizes fundament analysis. Long term investors buy stocks containing enormous dividends pay-out and regularly release or sell them after several years when the stocks have passed through several fluctuations while short berm traders usually utilize technical analysis. Such traders o did not buy or keep goods for years, but instead, they focus more on short term profits.
5. Fundamental utilizes the intrinsic value of stock got when one analyses income statements like cash flow management, profit margins, and returns on equity. They predict the future of the market. A technical analysis, depend on a chart, technical indicators, resistance, and support to analyze future trend patterns.
6. In fundamental analysis, no assumptions are made while assumptions like similar price trends are not news, in technical analysis
7. Fundamentals analysts don't need to go back to history to find to discover past prices and the fluctuations incurred. However, technicians trade re-occurs, and the possibility of history repeating itself is high.

So which analysis techniques should you choose?

Most analysis on street walls prefers fundamental analysis to technical analysis. Both technical and fundamental have their advantages and disadvantages. But a good investor will point out that their combination of both the two, end up producing t exceptional results.

Risk management

Knowledge of both fundamental and technical approach can help to handle any risk involved in a trade. Economic can tell if the attitude of particular market changes, but fails to inform you when the view of the market is wrong. Technical analysis helps you manage risk as you can view on the charts and can help you revise a market view.

Also, a combination of the two analyses can confirm specific trends. When, most people in a country expect a higher interest rate, but it doesn't manifest, then that countries' currency would likely decrease in value. Furthermore, When the currency continues rising, there could be a possibility of other factors involved rather than the interest rate. A technical trader can use the way markets reacts to fundamental news to their advantage

Partying shots

When marketers try to focus on future price movements, they use fundamental analysis to look at issues such as political developments and economic data.; they use technical analysis to read charts and interpret price movements or instead come the two. That what, you need to do a trader.

Chapter 5: Tools, Indicators, and Patterns of Trading

Tools of trade

This is a term used to help a person decide the kind of property they should use to earn and make a living. According to bankruptcy law, the exemption for tools of the trade is usually determined by the state in the state exemption statutes. The exemption can also be determined by federal law in the federal bankruptcy exemptions. The period of time in which a person lived in a state before filing could also be a determinant of the exemption. Lawyers assist their clients to understand which properties are exempt and the exemptions apply.

Anything a person can prove they use as a tool for trade is marked as a separate exemption from assets they own. This means that a person can be allowed an exemption for households separately from assets they use to make a living. One person may provide their vehicle as a property they own while another may produce their vehicle as a taxi which earns him his daily bread.

Having the right tools for trading will guarantee success for anyone starting. An experienced trader may not really be concerned about the tools they use but for beginners, the tools count.

Examples of Tools Used for Trade.

- Light speed financial broker – here a broker or a group of brokers breaks into different groups of specialization. The specialization is determined by the services they offer and the financial instrument used. The options for these brokers are Forex, stocks, long term investing and scalping brokers. Light speed brokers are very convenient for day time traders because of their direct accessibility and fast executions.
- Trade ideas stock scanning software – after establishing a good broker, the next step is finding the stock to trade with. The ability to determine stocks before they make a big move is what determines a more profitable trader. Trade ideas software helps in stock scanning for volume spikes, HOD movers to establish the gainers and the losers and things like that. This is the best software there is that scans the market and finds the winning stocks.
- signal charting – the third step is getting high-quality charts. The broker you chose makes come his standard charts. Those will work for you for some time until you decide to use ones that allow you to draw and write

formulas. Signal allows one to run charts on 8 monitors without time delay. This is advantageous to people who like observing several stocks at once. it also allows installation of custom scripts. Custom scripts can be used as custom indicators for reversals and drawing support and resistance lines.

- Breaking news provider – every morning, a trader should start by reviewing the market. After the review, you look at the catalyst to determine why stocks are moving higher. Reasons for the stocks could be moving up in consideration to the market, or a strong sector while other times it may be a unique catalyst like earnings. Breaking news provide the headlines for when the stocks are spiking.
- TAS market profile – this software is best in helping make trade decisions. It has several tools in it. Among them is a TAS scanner which allows one to observe stocks moving at different timings with different levels of buying and selling.

Having the right tool may not guarantee success in the trading world but it will give the right directions that will help make trading easier. The right tool will also provide an advantage for a trader over other traders who do not have the tools.

Indicators of Trade

This is a measure or gauge of trade that allows analyzing of prices and provides trade signals. Indicators provide trade signals that alert a trader when it is time to trade. Day trading indicators are not to be used as the only plan. They should be used along with a well laid out though to make it a useful trading tool. No matter the kind of trade one is involved in, having many trading indicators may bring inconsistency with trading decisions due to the complexities involved. Keeping it simple could simply be the trick to making clear and less stressful trading decisions.

Trading indicators should not, therefore, be taken as the only method relied on trading. However, using indicators alongside other trading variables may come in handy. Getting rid of the many indicators helps traders have a simplistic approach to the market.

Role of Technical Indicators

- Get the direction trend
- Determine the momentum or lack of momentum in the market
- Determine if and if not, the market is growing
- Get the volume to determine how popular a market is with traders

Getting the same type of indicators that on the chart that give the same information is where the issue is. This is because you may give conflicting information or get more information than you may be stressful. The main shortcoming of most indicators is that since they are gotten from price, they delay the price. There are rules that one can use to determine useful indicators for day trading, swing trading, and position trading. This include among others:

Choosing one trend indicator such as moving average and one momentum trading indicator is the simplest rule.

Knowing well the perimeters you want to investigate before you decide on the trading indicators which you will use on your charts. Then know well the indicator you chose in terms of how it works, calculations it does and the effects it will bring for your trading decisions.

Indicators work only depending on how they are incorporated into the trading plan. Some indicators like MACD and CCI are best at calculating information. Others like alligator indicator are fast at showing a market that is trending and ranging. Other indicators will show directions and act as entry and exit signals of trade. The usage of a basic indicator along with a well laid out trading plan by back, forward and demo can you put you ahead of trade with many complicated indicators. Netpicks offers systems that test trade plans, prove trading systems and trading indicators.

Threat of Optimization

There is a hindrance or barriers for when one is searching for trading indicators that work for one's style and trading plan. Most systems sell standard indicators that are fine-tuned to show successful results from the past. This is a disadvantage since it does not take into account the market changes. Using the standard settings for all indicators help avoid over-optimization trap which helps a trader not to focus on today's market progress and miss on the future.

Best Technical Trading Indicators

For day trading, a trader should test several indicators individually then later as a combination. One may end up with say 3-5 good ones that are evergreen and decide to switch off depending on the market at that particular day or the asset trading.

Regardless of the type of trade, day, Forex or futures the idea is to keep it simple with the indicators. Use one indicator per category to avoid repeating the same thing and distraction.

Combining Indicators

Combining pairs of indicators on the price chart helps to identify points to initiate trade. A good example is a combination of RSI and moving average convergence which combined suggest and reinforce a trading signal. When choosing sets it's important to find one indicator considered a leading indicator and another that is a lagging indicator.

Leading indicators show signals before the forms for entering trade has been made. Lagging indicators on the other hand show signals after the formation have happened. Therefore, lagging indicators can confirm leading indicators and help a trader from trading on wrong signals.

Choosing a combination of pairs that include indicators of different types instead of the same type is highly advisable. It does not make sense to observe a combination of the same type of indicators because they will still give the same information.

Multiple Indicators

Using multiple indicators boosts trading signals and may increase chances of telling out false signals.

Refining Indicators

It is important for a trader to take note and record the performance of the indicators they are using. Knowing the weaknesses of an indicator to determine if it gives a lot of false signals, if sometimes it fails to signal or if it signals too late or too early is essential. Knowing these things about the indicator will help determine what the indicator is best suited for. You may find that the indicator is suited for Forex instead of stocks while you thought it was just ineffective. This might help you decide if you want to trade the indicator for another or to just simply change how it's calculated. Doing this refining, will help an indicator work best for you, and also for you to find the best indicator for different types of trading.

Patterns of Trade

This is generally how trade takes place. It is the movement of price against a specific period of time. Patterns of trade are made of charts drawn in lines to connect proportional prices like the closing dates for a number of days.

Hammer Patterns

This is a reversal candlestick pattern that happens at the bottom of the depression. It is created when the open, high, and close prices are about the same price and a lower long shadow twice the length of the main body happens. In other words, hammer candlesticks form when shares fall from the opening prices due to pressure caused in selling. But then they manage to cover most losses experienced within the trading period.

Even when a hammer pattern is a single candle, an observation of the surrounding candles within that single stick is needed to confirm if it is indeed a hammer candlestick pattern.

If the hammer candlestick pattern forms in a depression, it is regarded as a market depression or support.

Verification Signals

- When the candle has a long lower shadow, there is a high chance of price reversal.

- When there is a lot of trade volume the day the hammer forms, it probably means a blow off in the trade.

- When the candle has a gap from the previous day closing price, it means that a strong reversal is expected to happen because the price opened higher a day after the hammer.

- A green candle will show the sign of a bull while a red sign will show the sign of a bear.

The Inverted Hammer Pattern

This candlestick is formed after depression and is a sign of a trend reversal. It looks like the reverse of a hammer candlestick pattern and its formation indicates an uptrend called a shooting star. If there is a downtrend and an inverted hammer with the sign of a bull is formed, it means that the prices delayed the upward move by a high increase during the day. Then the sellers made the prices push back near the open. Prices having increased show the bulls trying to overpower the bears. The next day determines if the prices go higher or lower and their observation is very important. The bullish pattern is a continuous pattern that represents a fall in the market after a strong unexpected move. The bullish pattern does not necessarily require the use of an indicator because it is itself a price action.

The bullish flag pattern is a strong technical pattern in that it has the ability to form in the shortest time frame of a minute up to a whole monthly chart. This pattern is constructed in two sections; the first is a powerful sustained rally while the other one is that, it has a tight range that is contained in two parallel lines.

There has been an immense growth in the global economy over the years. This has resulted in a change in the pattern trade. The changes include deindustrialization, the participation of communist countries and the emergence of India and China.

Although growth has been affected by short term changes due to the economic cycle, the value of trade has immensely improved. Globalization is taking over. Trade openness has also increased in most countries as an effect of globalization.

Chapter 6: Scalping Strategy

Scalping is a very fast-paced trading strategy and can be difficult for a beginner to learn. However, it's not impossible. Like the other trading strategies discussed, you want to ensure you are comfortable and understand the strategy before making a trade. With this main step, you will be on your way to success. The main idea of scalping is you profit off small price fluctuations. This means you will make quick and multiple trades throughout the day. Most people are full-time traders, but there are a few part-timers. This type of trading typically happens during the busy hours of the forex market, which is Monday to Friday from about 9:00 a.m. to 4:00 p.m. eastern time. A part-time trader might trade from 9:00 a.m. until around noon, when the market tends to quiet down for a bit. A full-time trader will work throughout the day, from 8:00 a.m. to around 4:00 p.m. eastern time.

Because these trades are small, traders will hold dozens of trades within their portfolio. This allows them to build a profit that can reach hundreds of dollars in a single day. Scalping traders don't often show patterns. They will make one trade within a few seconds and keep the next one for a few minutes. Sometimes, though rarely, they will keep some trades for a couple of hours.

Is Scalping Trading Right for You?

As a beginner, you want to make sure you can handle the fast-paced scalping trading. There are a lot of details that go into this type of trading because you need to quickly find the best time to make a trade. This can be a highly stressful environment, especially if you have dozens of stocks you are watching. Remember, you need to control your emotions. When you become stressed, your emotions can easily take over, which can cause you to make mistakes.

If you aren't interested in long-term trading, scalping is a strategy to look at. Scalping trading is often thought of as a subtype of day trading but focuses on the minute-by-minute charts. For example, a scalping trader is not going to look at the monthly or even weekly charts. They will focus on the one- to five-minute charts.

If you are interested in higher risk and can handle stress, you might look into scalping trading. However, scalping trading is something you might look into overtime. You can always start with day trading and then find you are more interested in scalping.

If you are interested in scalping trading, you might want to think about trying a different strategy or using simulation trading before you use real currency.

How to Apply Scalping Trading

One of the biggest factors to make scalping successful is to keep your gains bigger than your losses. It doesn't matter what type of trading you use; whether it's position, swing, day, or scalping, you will have losses and gains. When you are a long-term trader, you can find more losses and wins within your trades even if you have built a lot of capital. When you are scalping, you will see more wins than losses, but you need to make sure your strategy works in a way that will give you more capital. Long-term traders will gain a large capital with one trade. Scalping traders will gain a small capital with a trade. For example, position traders might receive a $3,000 capital from one trade they held for six months. A scalping trader will receive a total of $3,000 by combining capital from dozens of trades.

A Couple Types of Scalping

1. One type is market making, which is when a trader places a bid for a specific currency. The trades used for this strategy don't move too much, which means there is typically no chance of a large price increase. This is also one of the most challenging strategies with scalping because you need to compete with principal traders who focus on market making. They will usually have higher bids, which means you are more likely to lose the chance at the trade.

2. The second strategy closely follows the most common form of trading, which is when you purchase one pair and exit at the best possible moment for the highest profit. For scalping traders, they will exit when the first signal is noted. Usually, scalpers have a few signs that allow traders to know when the best times to enter and exit are.

Pros and Cons of Scalping Trading

Pros

1. It can be an exciting way to trade.

2. There are a lot of investments that show trading signs throughout the day, which gives you a lot of options for trades.

3. You don't need to focus on a lot of analysis. Scalping traders will mostly focus on technical analysis.

4. Scalping trading limits risk since you hold a position for a short a time span as possible.

Cons

1. Many trends continue over a long period. You are unable to take part in this profit as a scalping trader.

2. Negative news can be unexpected. You might have a position in your portfolio that is hit by negative news. This means will be an unusually high trading volume that can give you a potential loss.

3. You need to pay close attention to the market during the busiest hours. All your trades have to be closely managed throughout the day.

4. Scalping trading can be extremely stressful, which can bring your emotions into your decisions.

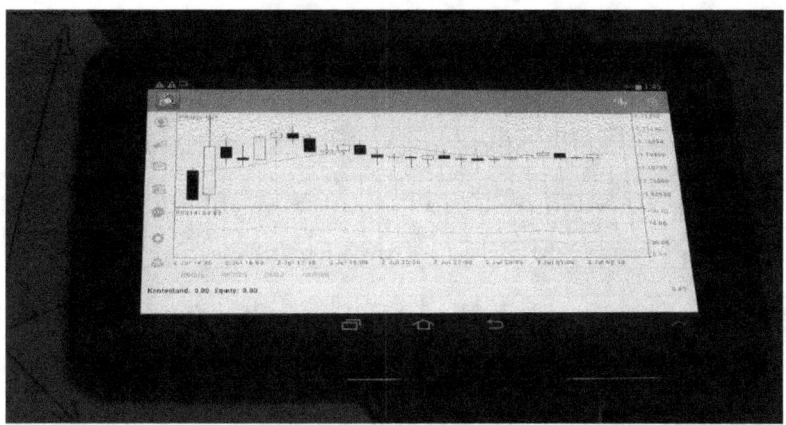

Tips for Beginners

Understand Technical Analysis

Technical analysis focuses on the strengths and weaknesses of price movements and other trading signals (Hayes, 2019). It can help you decrease some of the competition you will encounter as a trader. This is a topic you should consider learning while completing your research.

Stick to One Scalping Strategy

Earlier I discussed three different strategies that scalping traders use. While there are more, it is essential that you pick one strategy to stick with. This doesn't mean it's the only strategy you know; it's the one that works best for you.

The biggest reason you want to stick to one strategy is that it will allow you to maintain a sense of consistency. You will be able to learn everything you can about that specific strategy so you can become a master and be successful. Due to the fast-paced nature of scalping, you want to ensure you don't find yourself struggling during the wrong moment. Understanding one strategy will make sure you don't fall into this trap.

Make Sure You Are Comfortable

As humans, we often take on too much. We believe we can handle a situation and may quickly find ourselves in over our head. This doesn't mean you won't be a successful scalping trader; it can cause you to make too many mistakes. While mistakes happen, you also want to do whatever you can to limit your risk. Having too much risk, being uncomfortable about trading, and not understanding scalping can lead to significant capital loss. In fact, you can find yourself in debt as a trader. Don't feel that you can take on the trading world too early in your game. It is always best to start off slowly and take the time to learn everything you can.

Use Simulation Trading

As stated before, simulation trading is making real-time trades without real money. This is a great step for beginners because it will allow you to get a realistic view of the trading world. You can see how fast trades are made, how easy it is to gain a profit, and how quickly you can lose your capital. Learning this firsthand is a great experience. Furthermore, you can make mistakes without worrying about losing your money.

Limit Your Distractions

Forex scalping traders often work from home as trading is their full-time job. The downside is home often holds a lot of distractions, from watching your television to relaxing in your comfortable chair. This can cause problems as a trader because you can become more focused on your favorite television show than the market. It is important to ensure all your focus remains on the market when you are working. This will keep you from making mistakes and missing the best time to make a trade.

Chapter 7: What Are the Most Popular Forex Trading Styles and Strategies?

There are many ways of making money in the forex market. Choosing a style of operating is a stumbling block for many traders. This chapter is going to list out the various ways you can trade and also give you a strategy that works for that style. You can use these strategies to generate potentially profitable entry signals, but remember, profitability is a function of your risk math.

Having said that, let's look at the different styles of trading.

Day Trading

Day trading is the most popular form of trading out there and with good reason. You see, the market exists on a number of time frames, ranging from the monthly all the way down to the one minute. These charts capture price movement in those time frame intervals, and you can align your trading to these levels in order to capture price moves.

Day trading refers to holding a position for less than a day. In the case of the FX market, this refers to the 24-hour day which happens to be quite long. Usual time frames for day trading are the 30-minute charts and below. Day traders can also operate on a session-by-session basis where they exit their positions at the end of a particular session. This makes sense for crosses where volumes are bound to decrease at certain times.

This strategy calls for simply buying or selling at the relevant s/r levels on a chart.

USDSGD

Price here is represented via candlesticks, which are a Japanese form of representing price. Each candle or bar represents thirty minutes worth of price action since this is a thirty-minute chart, called M30. The horizontal lines represent important s/r levels. The lower s/r levels are a zone, and notice how price reacts to it when it first approaches the level after the initial swing point. This reaction is denoted by the first circle. The swing point prior to it was significant because it created a new high. After this bounce, the price went sideways for a bit before testing this level again, this time for longer. Notice how it didn't come back to exactly the level?

Well, this is a quirk of the USDSGD, and it sometimes behaves this way. If you had run simulations on this pair, you would have known that the pair requires a wider entry zone than most. Therefore, the second circle also provides us with a valid entry, even if it doesn't hit the s/r zone exactly.

As price moves past the previous highs, notice how it retests them before moving even higher. Remember the lesson from spotting s/r levels? Notice that price hit the previous high twice before testing the level below. It seems natural that price will bounce back and test this prior high zone before moving even higher.

As you can see, all trades lasted for less than a day if you were targeting a 2R trade. You could choose to let it run, but remember that the volumes of this pair would have decreased significantly outside the Asian session and volatility would have increased, thanks to a lack of liquidity.

The key to making this strategy work is to spot and trade s/r levels well. As mentioned earlier, this takes a lot of practice. A common pitfall of this strategy is to pay heed to wrong levels and to attempt trades from weak levels for fear of missing out. As you can see, there is no huge secret to this strategy, and it doesn't call for complicated lines or calculations.

You just see what's in front of you and trade. That's it!

Swing Trading

Swing trading is a method where you hold your position for longer than a day but up to a week. Common swing trading time frames are the one hour (H1), four hour (H4), and daily (D1). The daily provides very few opportunities to swing trade. As such, the H1 and H4 are the best time frames for this.

Day trading tends to have a fast pace since the price intervals are so low. If you're trading the five-minute chart (M5), the chart is changing every five minutes, and you need to assess what's going on. In contrast, the H1 and H4 change at a far slower pace, and you have more time to digest information.

This is why a lot of beginners prefer to swing trade since it has the right balance of speed—so you never get bored—and feedback—since it gives you a good number of opportunities despite the lack of speed. Swing trading also suits those who have full-time jobs. In an earlier example, I outlined how you could trade in the morning and after work.

Well, trading the four-hour charts provides an excellent way for you to carry this out. There are just six four-hour bars per day. Therefore, it becomes far easier to check-in after long intervals throughout the day since not much is changing. Often you will find that the chart looks the same and that it only begins to change after a few days. This makes it very easy to stay in touch with what is happening.

Before we get into a perfect swing trading strategy, I'd like to take some time to provide a brief primer on candlesticks.

Candlestick Basics

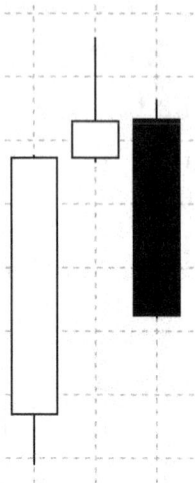

Candlesticks

The first two are bullish candles (or bars). The third one is a bearish bar. So what makes a candle bullish or bearish? Well, a bullish candle implies that during the time frame the candle covers, the price finished higher (closed) than where it began (opened). Thus, a bullish candle has its close higher than its open.

The situation is inverted with bearish candles, with the close being lower than the open. The color of the candle's body tells us whether it is bullish or bearish. In this case, the white candles are bullish and the black candles are bearish. The bodies of these candles have wicks and tails sticking out above and below them. What are these?

Well, price fluctuates constantly, as you know. A tail below the candle body implies that price went as low as the extent of the tail. A wick above the candle body, like in the second candle, implies that price went as high as the extent of the wick before closing where it did.

These wicks and tails give us invaluable information as to price behavior. Consider the second candle. We can see that it is preceded by a huge bullish candle which means that buyers were very strong. However, the second candle shows us that despite being bullish, the sellers came back in quite strongly. How do we know this?

Well, this is what the wick tells us. The bulls tried pushing the price higher, but the bears rejected this push, and this produced the wick on top. Notice how the next bar resulted in price falling strongly. Bars that have small bodies and large wicks or tails are considered strong signals of a change in price direction. By using these, we can develop pretty profitable strategies to trade the markets. Let's look at one now.

Trading with Candlesticks

First off, when using this strategy, you need to determine which way prices are headed. Up, down, or sideways. Then, find signals that affirm entries in the direction price is headed.

In such an environment, it makes no sense to try and go long since we'll just be putting ourselves against the majority of the market. There's not much benefit to being an outsider when it comes to trading, and profits are generated by figuring out which way the market is headed and joining it.

The bar highlighted within the circle is an example of a good entry signal to join the downtrend. The bars within the rectangle are examples of invalid bullish signals. Yes, price did go up soon after, but notice how soon it was rejected back down. There's no chance you would have been able to make money here.

Entering short at the circle would have been far more profitable for you, and price would have hit your target easily.

Trend Trading

Trend trading is a versatile strategy that can be used on any timeframe. The premise of this is quite simple. Trends exist in every time frame, and they tend to last a while. By entering trends and riding them to their end, you can take advantage of this fact. Trend trading is not an easy way to trade though and requires you to apply a lot of subjectivity, especially when it comes to assessing the current strength of the trend.

A Common Trend

Looking left to right, we can see that price is tilted upward, but we can also see that there are multiple times when price becomes quite bearish and moves downward quite strongly. So, what do we do in such a situation? One solution is to take the help of an indicator.

The 20 EMA is one such indicator. EMA stands for the exponential moving average. This indicator calculates the average closing price of the previous 20 bars and then draws a curve through them. You can draw EMAs for any number of periods you choose. The EMA curve often smoothes out a lot of price action, and it can be useful to make sense of what's going on.

Furthermore, the 20 EMA also proves useful as a dynamic s/r level when trends are extremely strong. The reason for this is that a lot of professional traders use this as an indicator. Moving averages, in general, can be thought of as good indicators of trend.

In such environments, the price is moving in a particular direction but doesn't do so for very long. There is a dominant direction, long in this case, but with significant bearish pressure. So it is imperative that you get in and out quickly. The EMA crossover strategy helps with this.

EMA Crossover

When price acquires momentum prior to a big move, the EMA5 picks this up quicker than the 20EMA and thus crosses it. Every time the EMA5 crosses the EMA20 from below to above it, this is called a crossover, and we can surmise that price is looking to move upward. The minute this crossover happens, we can look to enter and aim for a target to be hit to make a profit.

Well, the dominant trend is bullish in this case. Notice how just one portion of bearish movement gives us time to make a profit. We don't know this in advance and taking bearish crossovers would have resulted in losses for us.

The point is, always trade with the dominant trend. The circles indicate entry points for bullish crossover, and as you can see, all of them would have resulted in at least a 2R target being hit. The thing that really turbocharges a trend following strategy is to hold onto your positions as long as the trend exists. This is why trend following is a more advanced trading strategy. You need to figure out the exact environments where it is profitable to hold onto your positions for longer and where you need to simply take advantage of short-term movements.

The best way to practice trend trading is to seek to take advantage of short-term movements first. Once you can do this well, simulate and demo holding onto your positions for longer and see if you can make money this way. I suggest simulating at least 1,000 trades to see if you can make it work.

Trend trading can be extremely profitable, but you need to ease into it in a structured manner.

Intraday Trading

Within the stock market, intraday trading is also referred to as scalping, where traders hold onto positions for extremely short periods of time. Thanks to the longer opening hours of the FX market—perhaps lack of closure is a better phrase—intraday trading is actually more feasible here than with stocks.

While you can hold positions for extremely short periods of time, this is isn't advisable for reasons I've highlighted previously. In addition to squaring up against the heaviest hitters of the industry, your broker will also take a dim view of this sort of trading. This is because the shorter your holding periods are, the greater the chances of a price discrepancy happening with your trades.

Scalpers, traders who practice scalping, usually hold onto positions for less than a minute. During peak hours, this isn't a problem for brokers since liquidity is ample. However, if a scalper operates during off-peak hours in an instrument, the liquidity is going to be less and the chances of receiving a bad price increase. Thus, while the broker is still reconciling the initial trade, the trader has already closed their position on the terminal, leading to a mismatch between the trader's terminal and the broker's books.

In this day and age, this isn't an issue, and the discrepancy is soon settled. However, if this happens during a high volatility event, such as during an announcement of some kind, the broker's risk exposure becomes far too much, and this is why they clamp down on this sort of thing from the start.

However, you can practice intraday trading by trading within sessions. Each session lasts around eight hours, so this is hardly a small period of time. In fact, intraday trading in forex is equivalent to day trading in stocks. This strategy works best with pairs that are especially active during a particular time period and are inactive for the rest of the day.

You can also choose to trade the overlap sessions, or when Asia and London are online at the same time, which lasts three hours, and the New York-London overlap, which lasts four hours. These four hours are the most heavily traded, so trading just these hours on a lower time frame will give you exposure to good volatility and liquidity at the same time.

Given the shorter holding times, you need a strategy that will give you a good number of entry signals as well as inform you of changing market environments quickly. For this purpose, we can use the parabolic SAR indicator.

Parabolic SAR

The SAR in the indicator's name stands for stop and reverse. When the dots are above the price, this is a bearish indicator and dots below are bullish. You need to understand how to trade the SAR properly in order to interpret its signals, and the place to begin is to consider the market's direction.

When the price is moving sideways, you can take both bullish and bearish signals, but when price acquires a direction, it is best to stick to the trend's direction instead of trading both sides of the market.

As you can see, this is the M15 on the USDSGD, so the number of signals that are being generated are quite large. At this rate, trading just one instrument, you'll end up with at least 2-3 trades per session.

Fundamental Trading

While it is difficult to trade fundamentals in FX, it isn't entirely impossible. In fact, some of the biggest profits in FX are made by those who trade macroeconomic fundamentals. Doing so requires a keen understanding of the economic machine, though. For example, George Soros' famous bet against the pound is an example of a fundamental trade. The traders who profited from the SNB's decision to remove the peg to the euro were also betting on fundamental factors carrying through.

Providing a strategy to trade this way is a bit impractical. You will need to understand the various economic factors and how they relate to one another. Given the interconnectedness of the FX market, a blip in one part of the world could result in a butterfly effect like a hurricane in another.

If you possess a keen curiosity for economic factors and how currencies affect the dynamic, then pursue this method of trading. When doing so, it might be best for you to trade around events since they produce large movements. Announcements of interest rates and unemployment numbers impact the economy directly, but their impact on currencies is usually a second or third-degree effect. Therefore, the chances of being wrong are high.

Chapter 8: A New Species, Cryptocurrency

One of the possibilities that I am going to invite you to explore is trading in cryptocurrencies. Why does one invest mainly in crypto and blockchain related assets? Because they truly believe they are one of the biggest revolutions undergoing in this very moment and that this is the perfect time to get involved before the market explodes.

Another reason that people like cryptocurrencies and their market is that they are extremely volatile and provide the average Joe the possibility to make serious money without investing a lot. It is not a secret, in fact, that every time the market starts to rise, people rush into the search for the "next big win" and the question that circulates is always the same: "What will be the next cryptocurrencies that will go to 'the moon'?"

The issue with cryptocurrencies is that being a market that is not yet regulated in several countries, the risk of pumps and dumps, manipulation and fraud are just around the corner. This is why I wanted to cover them in this book. In fact, since they provide a great opportunity, I am worried that a lot of people may get involved without knowing what they are doing and will lose a lot of money down the line. Here I want to show you what I do before putting your money in a particular coin.

Before getting started, here is a list of useful tools for the analysis of cryptocurrencies:

1. *Coincheckup.com - one of my favorite sites, offers much more data than other cryptocurrency monitoring sites;*
2. *Coinmarketcap.com - one of the oldest crypto price tracking sites, far more popular than CoinCheckup, but offers less data;*
3. *Blockfolio - another popular cryptocurrency tracker.*

Now let's get to the good stuff.

Step 1 - Understanding your risk profile

Many people will advise you to buy "low capitalization" cryptocurrencies and tokens (ie between 10 and 100 million dollars) because they have a greater opportunity for growth in terms of percentage.

Although this statement is relatively correct, you have to keep in mind that the smaller a coin is, the riskier it is to invest in it. Why? It is because the project has a much higher risk of failing.

In traditional investments, most people are happy to get an annual return of 3% to 4%; but they could be in serious financial difficulty if the invested capital is lost, so most of the time more well-known, safer and more stable securities are selected.

Other people would instead be satisfied only with an annual yield of 7% - 12%. These people could also be willing to lose all their investment if things go wrong. In their case, they would point to a higher risk given the economic attitude they have at the base.

These two different groups of people have different "risk profiles".

It is important that in any purchase you make in your life (even for something "concrete" like a car), you do so knowingly about the financial risk profile you can afford to take.

My personal opinion is that just because something has higher chances of performance does not mean it is the best choice. In particular, I have invested mainly in the top 5 coins in terms of capitalization, because they are the safest spot right now. However, I always allocate a small part of my portfolio, 10% to be precise, to low cap coins. How do I find the most promising one? Here is what I do.

Step 2 - Identification of new coins or tokens

There are three main ways I usually use to find the "new" coins or tokens:

1. Through the posts of the Bitcointalk.org forum, more precisely in the section "Announcements (Altcoins)";

2. In the subreddit / r / cryptocurrencies;

3. In the "Newly Added" sections of CoinCheckup and "Recently Added" by CoinMarketCap.

Each of these is a great resource to discover interesting coins with great return potential over a shorter period of time. As already said, I only put in a maximum 10% of my capital into these underrated projects.

With every investment comes the possibility to get scammed and in the crypto world happens more often that I would like to see. During the last three years of experience, I have developed a series of principles that I follow in order to avoid being scammed. Here is what will make me decide NOT to invest in an asset.

Step 3 - Exclusion of coins and useless tokens/scams

One of the first things I do when I look at new projects is to subject them to very strict criteria to remove "fluff" projects from the list. In particular:

1. I do not trade cryptocurrencies in industries and sectors that I do not understand;

2. I do not trade cryptocurrencies whose teams are inactive in social media communication;

3. I do not trade cryptocurrencies whose start-ups/associations/companies are registered in countries where I cannot validate a solid corporate entity;

4. I do not trade cryptocurrencies if I cannot find the team members (with particular attention to the founder) on LinkedIn and validate that they are real profiles;

5. I do not trade cryptocurrencies whose teams adopt spamming strategies and do aggressive and noninformative marketing campaigns on social and non-social channels;

6. If a team is building a brand-new technology, I do not trade the cryptocurrency/token unless there is a detailed technical document explaining how it works;

7. If a cryptocurrency has a pre-ICO with a discount, I tend not to trade it. If I did, it would only be in the case where the discount compared to the public ICO is minimal and the amount purchased is "locked" for

a significant period of time (to avoid massive dumps after the public ICO);

To help me with the process, I also use a series of questions that allow me to get more in depth and realize the true fundamental value of a coin. In particular, I really like to ask myself the following questions:

- Would I use this cryptocurrency as an end user, at least in the foreseeable future?

- Would I pay that price as a user?

- Does this project require the development of a new technology?

- What is the team's experience in this determined direction? Have they already managed a successful company? What was the performance of this company?

- Does the team have the ability to develop this technology? Are engineers and developers recognized in this sector? Do they have product managers and customer support?

- Is it clear how the project will generate users/customers?

- Why are they using the blockchain? Do they really need it or do they use the term "blockchain technology" to hype their project up just because everyone else is talking about it?

Pay attention to absolutist statements. Each project has negative aspects and consequences, a real project will be realistic in delineating them, especially the latter.

If I can see that each question has a positive answer, I will then allocate a part of my portfolio. I always trade for a slightly longer term and I am willing to stay in a coin for at least one year. If for any reason, I do not feel confident enough to put money into a project for at least 52 weeks then that means that it is probably wise to look at another one.

Predicting with utmost accuracy the next cryptocurrency that will make the boom is almost impossible, out there are so many projects based on nothing that still capitalize tens of billions of dollars; in the same way, there are dozens of serious projects that deserve more, but they failed to stand out and gained visibility as compared to others. The golden rule is that which applies in every financial market: diversify. By diversifying between several coins, you reduce the risk.

Chapter 9:
How to Develop a Winning Routine

A lot of information has been given to you throughout this book. It is a lot to digest, but there are some easily followed tips and tricks you can use to develop a winning routine. Remember that consistency and discipline are what produce profits. You need to simply execute the basics well, and this chapter is going to provide you with tips as to how to do that.

Establish Specific Goals and Objectives

What is it that you wish to achieve with your trading? Why do you want to trade successfully in the first place? Trading can be a dull and boring thing to do at times. The movies often portray trading as being something that is fast-paced and adrenaline-filled, but this isn't quite true.

Most of the time you're going to be simply watching and waiting. During these times, it can seem as if you're not making any progress and that you're simply wasting your time. So how are you going to make sure you remain on track? By using your passion, of course. You need to tap into the reason you're trying to learn to trade in the first place.

There is a lot of money to be made in trading, but why do you want this? Money for its own sake is not going to keep you motivated for long. This is because once you have enough money to be comfortable, you'll lose motivation. The threshold for you to be comfortable is a lot lower than you thinks, so don't think that you need to make a million per year to hit this level.

Always connect the money you wish to make back to your true purpose, and you'll find that things will work for you and that you'll never lack motivation. Is setting a goal to make X dollars per month or year a good one? I'd advise against setting a monetary goal like that.

The reason is that you're not in control of your results in trading. I mean to say that you don't know in advance how your odds are going to play out and in what distribution. Therefore, it is best to tie your goals to the execution of your process. If your goal is to make sure you follow your risk plan, then you'll make sure that you're maintaining your risk math at all times. Setting a goal that measures your ability to pull the trigger and enter trades is another goal you can set.

You can set mental goals as well. Often traders will feel enormous amounts of pressure when in a position to make a profit and be done with it. Why is this? Well, it's usually because they don't understand the risk management side of trading and the full repercussions on what that means. In short, they're thinking like the gamblers and not the casino.

Take the time to set your goals and gear them toward mental outcomes and the execution of your process. You'll find that your results will take care of themselves.

Let Your Profits Run

Letting your profits run is one half of the method of increasing your profits. I've touched upon the way to do this in terms of execution already. So why am I mentioning it again? Well, aside from it being important, there is a mindset element to this which often gets ignored.

The sound of increasing profits is understandably attractive to a lot of traders, and having spent a lot of time and put in a lot of hard work to make some money, they rush into this aspect of trading without preparing the ground well in advance. The thing is that no matter how successful at trading you are, the work doesn't stop.

It's not as if you can stop being disciplined or stop logging your trades once you make money. If anything, the work becomes harder because you will be faced with even bigger challenges. It's a bit like going from high school varsity ball to the pro leagues. A pro has more things to deal with than a high school player.

Increasing your profit size and letting your trades run falls into this advanced skill category. Aside from evaluating the risk-reward on offer, you also need to call the market direction properly to make sure it hits your secondary target. This involves a lot of testing. A good idea is to set up a demo account where you trade the same instruments as in your live account. In the demo account, let your profits run, and at the end of a year, or after 500 trades, compare the two accounts and see which one made more money and why. Follow a structured path toward all improvements to make sure they actually stick.

Cut Your Losses Short

This is something even beginner traders can do and is actually far easier to do than letting your trades run for longer. The beginner way to cut your losses short is mostly mental. In other words, beginners will make mistakes such as entering incorrectly or taking wrong signals. If this is the case, don't remain in the trade. Simply close it as soon as possible and exit. Do not become an involuntary investor who waits for their trade to go back into the green. If you made a mistake, then get out even if it means taking a loss. Needless to say, honor your stop-loss levels in trades that are correct entries as well. Sometimes you'll have trades that you initially thought were going to be sure winners turn pear-shaped and head for a loss.

A huge mistake that traders make at this point is to remove the stop-loss order and give the trade some 'room to breathe.' This is the textbook play on how to lose money trading. Never bring your emotions into trading by falling in love with a trade idea. Remember the correct mindset to adopt when it comes to trading and execute it.

If your trade has approached its profit target and is 70% of the way there already, you can move your stop-loss level up to your entry point. Unless your profit level is really close by it is unlikely that price will dip back below your entry point and then go back up to hit your profit target. It will either hit it or it won't. So if it doesn't hit the profit level, exiting for a breakeven result is a good result.

Once your skills are more advanced, you will be letting trades run. You can consider trailing your stop by moving it past your entry point and locking in some profit. You can place it at predetermined R points, such as 1R, 2R, and so on. Remember to trail your stop at a good distance, though, since you need to give your trade room to move.

Avoid Too Much Risk

The risk that I've spoken of thus far has been of the mathematical variety, that is success rates and average wins and so on. There is a mental side to risk management as well. As much as you would like to deny it, life happens to all of us. There are times when we perform at our best, and there are times when we get exhausted and simply cannot come close to what we're capable of.

Trading is a mentally exhausting profession. It is unreasonable to think you can trade for all twelve months of the year and only take holidays when the market is closed. You need to live your life as normally as possible, and this begins with treating yourself well and making sure your health is on point, both mentally and physically.

Ignoring your health is taking on too much risk. Your brain needs to be fresh and healthy to function properly and to execute your trading strategy. Some people try to tough it out as if that's an intelligent thing to do. If you find that you need to use your will power to trade, you're doing it all wrong.

Trading should feel effortless and comfortable in order for you to succeed in the long term. If you find the need to motivate yourself constantly to sit in front of the screen, then it won't be long before you burn out. So always make sure your daily life's needs are taken care of before trading.

Trading is not a get rich quick scheme, and the last thing you should do is quit your full-time job to focus on trading full time. It will not work out for you because trading is not going to give you the money you need to take care of expenses at first. This will only put you in a bad place mentally, and you will never succeed as long as that state of affairs remains valid.

So always seek to reduce the pressure on yourself as much as possible. Make it as easy as possible for you to trade. Trading is tough enough, so don't place additional barriers in your path.

Educate Yourself

Committing to a lifelong program of self-improvement is the best way to make sure you stay ahead of the curve. The markets are dynamic, and the only thing that's constant is that they keep changing. Therefore, it is imperative that you keep educating yourself and keep working on improving your skills constantly. A lot of traders get lazy when they reach a certain level of income and begin to stray away from their path of discipline. Such traders will soon find that the markets begin to reclaim the profits the traders made, and before they know it, their systems don't work anymore, and they need to begin all over again.

This is usually the case with traders who follow mechanical systems. Traders often get lazy with these because there's no need to actually analyze the market. All they need to do is wait for a signal and enter.

Therefore, don't use such systems as a crutch. Always keep working on your skills and maintain your curiosity about the way the markets work. You'll find that this is the best way to become and remain successful.

Chapter 10: Manage Your Emotions with Trading Psychology

Emotions are at the core of the human experience. Our first line knee jerk reactions to experiences, people and phenomena are always on an emotional level. We can therefore not ignore the impact that emotions have on our ability to successfully navigate through life in terms of relationships, career, and business.

Emotional intelligence is now widely recognized as an instrumental factor for success both in the workplace and personal levels. The ability to not only recognize but also manage your emotions will go a long way in ensuring that the decisions you make are based on logic and not on emotional highs and lows. A key tenement of emotional intelligence is self-awareness. Self-awareness requires you to be aware of what you are feeling and also identify the trigger or triggers that make you feel a particular aware. To be self-aware you will need to practice self-analysis through reflection to identify the behavioral tendencies that you develop based on your emotional weather. While it may sound like a straight forward concept, emotional reactions occur on a subconscious level and you would be surprised at how many times we make emotion-driven decisions without even being aware of it.

The Basics of Trading Psychology

The ability to control emotions while trading can make the difference between success and failure in forex trading. Your mental state has a significant impact on the decisions that you make. This is especially true for a new trader in the forex market. Emotions can lead to greed, where you might end up taking unnecessary risks and ignoring your trading plan in order to make a quick buck.

Fear/Nervousness

Fear is a natural human emotion especially when we perceive a situation that could be damaging to either ourselves or our best interests. This holds for investors in different fields including foreign exchange traders. A common cause of fear in trading is when a trader has put too much of their capital on a trade or made a move on a volatile market magnifying their risk exposure and increasing the probability of losses.

Over-leveraging yourself, lack of a solid trading plan and improper execution of trading strategies can cause the trader experience fear of losing their trading capital and ending up in losses.

Greed/Overconfidence

Greed can be a result of impatience where a trader wants to realize huge returns within a short period of time or when a trader on a profitable streak becomes overconfident and tries to go for more and more profits. If you find yourself developing a tendency of preferring only trades that promise big returns you may be letting greed guide your trading.

While it is natural to want to make the most out of your investments if you find yourself constantly throwing caution to the wind and engaging in high-risk trades for a quick pay off you may be letting greed influence your trading experience and will likely end up incurring losses due to poor risk management.

Overconfidence can also result in poor decision making when trading. Markets can change rapidly due to any number of factors and a good streak can turn on a dime and that profits can rapidly turn to loss if you do not have effective stop and take profit mechanisms in place. Sloppy trading as a result of overconfidence can end a strong run.

Conviction/Excitement

Not all emotions can be classified as 'bad' for trading. Trading like any other venture requires an individual to have sufficient levels of self-motivation and drive to keep them going.

While good trades can also result in losses just like bad trades, the principle to work with is that you should be winning or losing on good trades.

Winning and Losing Mindsets in Trading

A successful trader realizes that success will stem from a winning mindset. To develop a successful forex trading mindset, it is important to deal with both profits and losses in such a way that they do not cause you to deviate from your trading plan and strategies.

A losing mindset will be characterized by;

- Lack of a trading plan. Trading without a solid plan is akin to gambling. A plan helps in mapping out your trading strategies and in avoiding poor decision making.
- Trading based on greed. We all want to make money, but letting greed drive your trading will cause more losses than profits.
- Overleveraging. It is tempting to over-leverage in an attempt to maximize on returns but you should remember that leverage multiplies your risk factor in much the same it does your profit.

Steps to Develop a Winning Mindset

1. Have Realistic Expectations

While forex trading can be lucrative, approaching it with a get-rich-quick mentality will decrease your chances of successful trading. Poor risk management in an attempt to make a lot of money in a short period of time is almost always a self-defeating strategy.

2. Trade with Money You Do Not Need to Live

When investing in any venture, it is wise to use money that you do not require for day to day living expenses. Trading capital should come from your disposable income. Trading with money that you need to live on will lead to severe emotional pressure which will, in turn, impact your trading decisions and is likely to result in losses.

3. Develop Patience

Successful traders understand the power of patience. When you are patient you will be able to stick with your trading plan and will not allow emotions such as greed or anxiety to influence your trading plan.

4. Understand That Trades Are Not Inter-Dependent

It is easy to be tempted to over trade after a losing trade or after a winning trade. This is because you will be trying to make up for lost money or trying to capitalize on a winning streak. In both these cases, you will have let the outcome of your past trade influence the next one. This is not a good trading strategy. Your last trade should have no impact on the next trade.

Every trade should be in keeping with your trading plan and strategy and not a reaction to your last trade. For example, if you just had three consecutive winning trades, do not risk an unusual amount on the next trade assuming that the fourth trade will be a success because the first three were successes. Similarly, losing a particular trade should not be taken as an indicator that you are on a losing streak. When you start basing your trades on your past trades then you are operating on emotion rather than a logical trading plan.

5. Have a Trading Plan

It is commonly said that failing to plan, is planning to fail. Forex trading is not exempt from this rule. Like any other venture, you should go into trading with clear goals and objectives as well as a road map on how to achieve them.

A trading plan will keep you on track and help you avoid making emotional and rash decisions. A trading plan does not need to be complicated to be effective, simply writing a plan of what your objectives for the next week or trading session are will keep you on track while making your trades.

Day Trading or Long-Term Trading?

Timing is a crucial factor in forex trading and results in different categories of trading depending on the length of the trades that are made. These categories of trading include;

- Day trading
- Long term trading
- Swing trading

Day trading

Day traders will typically trade based on the information they acquire from economic news releases. These economic releases cause significant moves in the forex market when they are met or exceeded and these moves, in turn, generate profits for day traders. The price volatility of a particular currency and its average daily range is an important element in day trading.

The allure of fast and quick money that is characteristic of day trading is what attracts most beginners to this type of forex trading. Proficient scalpers are able to make quick money even though they take more risks. The limited timeframe of the short term trades can effectively limit your risk exposure in the market since you are trading for a limited period.

Day trading is a high pressure and high-stress environment that can prove challenging for beginners because they have a limited window to turn a profit from their investment. This pressure can cause them to execute losing trades and they can end up losing their trading capital as a result.

In day trading, intra-day volatility affects not only the entry point, but it can also impact the exit point. When it comes to day trading and short-term strategies, good timing will be the primary determinant of your success or failure in trading.

Long term trading

Long term trading usually involves trading in the forex market by holding a trade position for an extended period of time. This period can range from a couple of weeks to months or years. Short-term price fluctuations and the economic news do not have as big an impact on long term trading as they do on short term trading.

Long term traders do not need to look at the market's daily basis because they make long term trades that remain in play for extended periods of time. This means that people with day jobs or other commitments can comfortably engage in long term trading because it does not require constant monitoring.

A trader can choose to have both short-term forex trades and long-term trades as part of a diversified investment strategy. It is important to note that while long term trading offers less action requires little daily monitoring, day trading is a fast-paced, active method of trading that requires a high tolerance for stress and pressure as well as constant vigilance.

Keep a Daily Diary

Keeping a trading diary is primarily used to help you in sticking to your trading plan and strategies. A trading journal is a mechanism that a trader can use in recording their past, current and intended trades. The data captured in the journal provides a means for self-evaluation in terms of the efficacy of the trading strategies used. When you come up with a good trading plan that is well documented, you will be in a position to effectively review your performance, plans, and strategies and determine what works and what doesn't.

The main objective of your trading diary is to allow you to have a detailed account of your trades and their performance in terms of profit or loss and to enable you to gauge the efficacy of your trading plan.

The Two-Part Journal

Your trading journal should:

- Give you a clear record of trades made.

- Have a clear indication of the strategies used to direct a particular trade.

This data will enable you to calculate the reliability of your trading system after observing several trades. When doing your analysis use data from similar strategies to avoid getting inconclusive results that can be caused by having multiple variables in your analysis.

In summary, your diary will serve as a;

1. Planning Tool

A good trade journal will have a record of your actual trade data as well as your intended trades. When you plan ahead for your trades you can put in place mechanisms such as stop loss and take profit limits.

2. Historical Record

Over a period of time of recording your trades in a journal, the journal will provide a historical perspective on your trading patterns. It will summarize all your trades and provide an insight into the state of your trading account.

3. Methodology Verification

A journal is an effective tool that you can use to verify your methodology. By studying your trades over a period of time you can easily determine which strategies deliver favorable results and which ones you need to change because they do not work well.

Chapter 11:
Risk management & Trading Plan

If you follow this technique, you surely will see your trading results change.

In the money management books, there are many fine words written, but then on the practical side, just a few of them can customize a method that can help formulate a trading technique. Don't you think?

I will explain to you another simple thing I use to be profitable over time, even in periods in which I can occur more losses than profits.

You will say: Impossible!

The trading signals you are learning have high-profit rates, but we need a risk management technique that maximizes our efforts and our work.

A trader who trades with a ratio of 90 wins and 10 losses, but who is not a good risk manager, with just a single loss operation he could end up giving back to the market all the work he has done!

This means that to be a professional trader it is not enough to have a good technique!

For every trade, we should know how much we are willing to lose.

If we have only a few trading signals, then it becomes simple to focus on the risk of our operation. Remember: before being good traders we have to be good risk managers, then we will become excellent traders.

When I see a good trade, I insert 3 different orders and I set up them like the following:

First order, automatically earns profit where the first key level will be.

Second order, automatically earns profit where the second key level will be.

Third order, automatically earns profit where the third key level will be but, usually, I do not insert the take profit, I just leave the order running.

When the first order earns at profit, I move the stop loss of the second and third order at price entry.

This means that the second and third order can have a zero gain that is also a zero loss.

This is the BREAK-EVEN POINT, and this is one of the most important techniques of the strategy.

Another point is that something everyone does, it is thinking about the percentage of risk in relation to capital.

We will match this percentage for the money we are willing to lose!

Psychologically, you'll see, it will be much more manageable and, it will maximize your profits!

So, the thing I suggest is to risk a percentage between 1% to a maximum of 2% per trade. Then our calculations will think only in cash!

So, making a practical example point by point, see here below:

5 PM. We open the chart and we look at this formation.

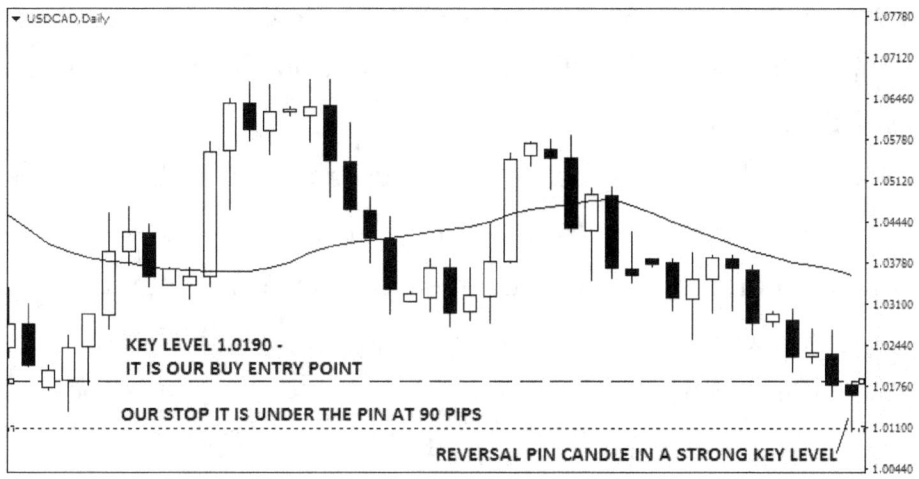

We then trade with a buying position at the break of the maximum of the daily inversion pin at 1.0190.

We take the signal against the trend only because it is on a strong key level of the chart.

Our stop loss, in this case, will be 90 pips below the minimum of the pin.

Instead of giving us a maximum percentage of loss in relation to the capital, we give ourselves a value in money (usually I always recommend a figure we emotionally attempt to leave to the market and which never exceeds 2% of the capital, as reported above).

For this trade, I want to lose a maximum of $100.

What will I do then?

I need to calculate how many lots I have to insert to lose only 100 American $.

As explained, the value of a pip for 1 lot is equal to 10 units of the value at the base of the cross we are trading.

So, in this case (USD/CAD), one pip of one lot is equal to 10 Canadian dollars.

Which is the conversion between the American Dollar and the Australian Dollar? At the moment 1 American Dollar is equal to 1.019 Australian dollars. This means that we are willing to lose 100 (American Dollar) x 1.019 = 101,9 Canadian Dollars.

Now I have to take the amount I am willing to lose, (Canadian) $101,9 and divide it by the pips of the entry setup.

Then: 101,9 (Canadian Dollar maximum loss) / 90 (pips - loss of our signal) = 1.13

For convenience, we round to 1.1, and this has to be divided for 10.

1,1/10 = 0,1

What does it mean?

This means I will open a position with 0.1 lots or 1 mini lot or 10 micro lots.

Because of the break-even point technique, I will then divide this value by 3 so as to place 3 different orders so:

0.1 / 3 = 0.36 lots (we round at 0.4 mini lost = 4 micro lots)

It seems complicated, but with a little practice, it won't be difficult at all.

Anyway, there is a lot of websites that can give you a hand to do this calculation.

Nowadays a lot of brokers have their calculator directly in their trading platform, so don't worry about this.

Anyway, I want you to learn how to do this by yourself so you can better estimate it all by yourself.

To better understand this, I will give you another example:

If our setup says we want to lose a max 100 American Dollar and our stop loss is equal to 150 pips then:

100 American Dollar = 101.9 Canadian Dollar (base of the cross)

101.9 Canadian Dollar / 150 Pips = 0.68 that we round for convenience to 0.7

0.7/10 = 0.07 – 0.07 / 3 (orders) = 0.02

This means I will open three orders of 0.02 lots = 0.2 mini lots = 2 micro lots.

I recommend you choose a broker who can give you the opportunity to use mini and micro lots so as to better divide the risk and operate better with this method, especially if you do not immediately have an amount in your portfolio around and over 10,000 $.

Let's now move on to the next step essential for being profitable.

I ALWAYS enter a trade to get a 1: 3 RISK-REWARD

Risk 1 to take 3.

Applying this rule to the example above, I will risk $100 to make $300.

Now let's see, 3 examples:

1st EXAMPLE

My trading operation has a 70% profit in a daily time frame.

So basically, we have 70% of winning trades and 30% of losses.

Initial capital 5,000$

1st trade	lost	100$
2nd trade	gain	300$
3rd trade	gain	300$
4th trade	gain	300$
5th trade	lost	100$
6th trade	gain	300$
7th trade	lost	100$
8th trade	gain	300$
9th trade	gain	300$
10th trade	gain	300$

After 10 trades, maintaining a risk-reward of 1: 3 we would have a portfolio balance of $ 6,800 or a gain of $ 1,800.

2nd EXAMPLE

My trading operation has a 50% profit in a daily time frame.

So basically, we have 50% winning trades and 50% losses.

Initial capital 5,000$

1st trade	lost	100$
2nd trade	gain	300$
3rd trade	gain	300$

4th trade	lost	100$
5th trade	lost	100$
6th trade	gain	300$
7th trade	lost	100$
8th trade	gain	300$
9th trade	lost	100$
10th trade	gain	300$

After 10 trades, maintaining a risk-reward of 1: 3 we would have a portfolio balance of $6,000 or a gain of $1,000.

3rd EXAMPLE

My trading operation has a 30% profit in a daily time frame. So basically, we have 30% winning trades and 70% losses.

Initial capital 5,000$

1st trade	lost	100$
2nd trade	lost	100$
3rd trade	gain	300$
4th trade	lost	100$
5th trade	lost	100$
6th trade	gain	300$
7th trade	lost	100$
8th trade	gain	300$
9th trade	lost	100$
10th trade	lost	100$

After 10 trades, maintaining a risk-reward of 1: 3 we would have a portfolio balance of $5,200 or a gain of $200.

As you may have understood, trading is a statistical job.

As you can see if I had a poor strategy with a 70% losing trade, but was operating with a trading plan that provides a risk reward of 1: 3, I still would have gained.

By implementing the technique described in this manual, with a good trading plan you can have a steady growth in your portfolio.

Obviously, the examples above show perfect math that hardly will be the same in the market: trading is not so perfect!

If next to this risk-reward plan for each trade you end up matching the technique of breaking-even, you will have satisfaction from the market and positive profit statistics!

Let's continue the previous trade on USD/CAD.

With this chapter, you are entering the mentality of a professional trader!

This chapter is probably the most important of the whole book, so please read it again two or three times so as to better memorize all the points.

Chapter 12: Common Mistakes and Tips for Beginners in Forex Trading

The forex market due to its low restriction makes the market one of the most available market in the world. With an internet connection, phone or computer, and some few dollars, you can begin trading in the market. However, because of its free accessibility does not mean it is easy to make huge returns. In this chapter, I will explore some common mistakes most beginners make in their quest to make a profit. When I started trading, I made some of these mistakes and you have the chance of learning from my mistake. For a fact, I will be saving you thousands of dollars you may have squandered.

Common Forex Mistakes

Mistakes in forex are unavoidable but there are always remedies to deal with such a situation. Before you consider plunging into trading, it is important to consider the following mistakes and do everything possible to avoid them in the future. Most people are persuaded to venture into forex trading with fantasies of getting rich overnight.

Undeniably, the opportunities in the forex market are innumerable for you to make money and live the lifestyle you want. Notwithstanding, the forex road is not an easy road to travel because it is full of bumps. If there is anything, I can assure you as a beginner is that you will struggle for various reasons including having a poor forex foundation, poor trading structure, and impatience.

These common mistakes cripple the confidence of most beginners. I can boast that you have a solid foundation if you went through the beginning of this book to the end. However, how you apply the principles in this book depends on you only. These mistakes are the reasons most traders consider the market a scam. I am sure your testimony will be different because you are learning from the best book on forex trading.

Tips for trading forex

Just as I promised you at the beginning of this book to help you avoid the mistake I made as a beginner, I have decided to compile most mistake beginners as you make. In this section, I will expound on the top trading tips you should inculcate into your trading and improve your performance.

Learning to trade successfully in the forex market is quite problematical for new traders. Most traders have the mindset of getting rich overnight, which is not something realistic. Forex trading can be prodigious particularly if you are a beginner and do not know the rules guiding the market. These tips will help you in your trading journey as a beginner. It is always advisable not to forget the basics because without them you will struggle in the market.

Pick your broker cleverly

If you can choose the right broker, then you are halfway done in the forex market. Before choosing any broker, it is important for you to review various brokers. Ensure to seek recommendations from professional traders and make your own research because some traders will recommend a particular broker because of their affiliate programs. Take your time as we have various fake brokers looking for traders like you to ripe off. Do not be moved by mouthwatering deals, rather look for an authorized broker with years of accomplishment.

Develop your strategy

A list of tips on forex trading is not complete without mentioning strategy. As a beginner, you need to create your own trading strategy that works for you. Every trader should know what to expect and get from the market. You should set a definite goal because it will help discipline yourself when trading.

Learn Slowly

Forex is not something you learn and stop over time. Every new skill requires consistent learning to grasp the basics. Additionally, you do not have to rush your learning process. Take your time slowly and begin by investing a little amount of money. Remember that slow and steady will win the race as a beginner.

Control your emotions

If you allow your emotions to guide you when trading, you will regret it later. I am not telling you that it is easy but you can control it. You need to stay rational in order to make wise choices during trading. If you let your emotions to rule over you, you are bound to expose yourself to pointless risks. Forex trading is risky but you can control the level of risk that can happen.

Do not trade if you are under stress

Hardly can you see someone who concentrates optimally when under stress. Traders who decide to do that will surely make an irrational decision, which will cost them money. Therefore, before thinking of trading, ensure to identify anything that will cause stress and eliminate them before it eliminates your forex account (do not mind me I am just joking but there is a sense to it). If you had a stressful day and still had to trade, consider taking a deep breath while allowing your mind to focus on what you are about to do. You can overcome stress in various ways such as exercising, sleeping, and listening to music, hanging out with friends. Whatever the situation is, find a solution to your stress and manage it effectively.

Never stop practicing

Do not neglect this tip because it is crucial to your success or failure as a forex trader. Hardly can you succeed on your first encounter in the forex market. Therefore, when you make your first mistake, do not relent because, with consistent practicing, you will be among the top traders. However, you have the adventure of using a demo account to perfect your skill.

Risk is part of the game

If you are not ready to risk, you are not ready for the forex market. Most brokers will advise you that trading is risky and you should accept that fact. If you think that in forex you are going to have a sweet ride, then you need a reality check. Additionally, I have seen mouthwatering advertisements promising you the "unpromising." Well, you should be realistic about your goals and strategies.

Patience is priceless

Do you remember the old adage? "True success is never instantaneous." That holds true in the forex market. It is the product of consistent planning and work, which many beginners tend to overlook. There is no easy path to making a profit in the market. Let patience have her way in you.

Upgrade your knowledge continuously

The more you trade, the newer things you learn. Improve your knowledge by looking at trends, analyzing news, and financial processes. Furthermore, do not neglect the fundamental basis you have learned. Significantly, you should study, practice, and continue this routine. A knife gets dull when it is left idle. Sharpen your trading skill with continuous learning and practicing.

Take breaks

All work and no play make Jack a dull student. You can take routine breaks especially when you are under stress. For those glued to multiple computer winds to analyze data from various source, it is important to take a break as you may feel pressured.

Trends are essential

Trends are important for any trader and you should not neglect them. The capability to identify these trends makes it a valuable investment for you. I understand there are various trends, it is important to ignore those that will lead to disaster. Trends give you a picture of what may come in the future. With this, you can prepare for the future.

Planning is a necessary ingredient

Forex trading is not sports betting where you gamble the team to win or score. Forex trading is a strategic game that requires painstaking planning and attention to evaluate your next move before taking action. Before starting any trade, formulate a plan that includes challenging questions like:

- What is my primary plan?
- What is plan B?
- What strategy should I employ?
- What are my loss and profit margins?

Understand the charts

You will trade in various markets and these require different information to analyze each trade. We have numerous tools you can use to make your trading easier. However, charts are time efficient and serve as the best option for beginners. You should not know them only, you should learn how to read and use them to your advantage.

Incorporate stop-losses in your trades

Setting stop-loss for trade is an efficient strategy to use when trading. With stop-loss, you minimize your risk and escape any trade that goes haywire. Additionally, avoid greediness by setting the maximum profit and loss range. Once you hit your target, you should avoid the trap of placing another trade.

Conclusion

Thank you for reading to the end!

Remember that the most important thing for your success is the combination of your win rate and the average win rate. Too many traders focus only on the win rate and not on the latter, thus resulting in a very warped view of what trading is all about. Always keep your risk per trade at a manageable level with the risk of ruin zero. If possible, fix your risk per trade a few levels below the threshold in order to account for miscellaneous mistakes you might make.

Follow the simulation, demo, and live framework to implement anything with regards to your trading. Always begin with simulation first to ramp up your screen time quickly. The more charts you expose yourself to, the quicker your skills will build. Track the relevant metrics of your trading system with the tools listed in this book and adopt a proactive approach to everything to do with your trading.

Remember to schedule regular breaks from trading, and don't trade if you're in a tough position mentally in your life. There is no need to become a slave to the market, and to think that the market is somehow going to get away from you if you don't trade is a mistake. Take the time to work on your skills during this off time and refine your strategies.

Your trading journal is a valuable tool when it comes to helping you improve. Treat the logging of your trades with discipline and do not slack in this regard when you begin to make money. Remember the things you track are the things you can improve. Lastly, I would like to wish you the best of luck and would like to thank you for taking the time to read this book. I hope it has been as much of a pleasure for you reading it as it has been for me writing it. It might seem frustrating at times, but trading really is a wonderful way to improve your life and that of your loved ones.

Give it the respect it needs, and you'll find yourself rewarded beyond your dreams. I wish you the best of luck once again!

© Copyright 2020 - All rights reserved.

The content contained within this book may not be reproduced, duplicated or transmitted without direct written permission from the author or the publisher.

Under no circumstances will any blame or legal responsibility be held against the publisher, or author, for any damages, reparation, or monetary loss due to the information contained within this book. Either directly or indirectly.

Legal Notice:
This book is copyright protected. This book is only for personal use. You cannot amend, distribute, sell, use, quote or paraphrase any part, or the content within this book, without the consent of the author or publisher.

Disclaimer Notice:
Please note the information contained within this document is for educational and entertainment purposes only. All effort has been executed to present accurate, up to date, and reliable, complete information. No warranties of any kind are declared or implied. Readers acknowledge that the author is not engaging in the rendering of legal, financial, medical or professional advice. The content within this book has been derived from various sources. Please consult a licensed professional before attempting any techniques outlined in this book.

By reading this document, the reader agrees that under no circumstances is the author responsible for any losses, direct or indirect, which are incurred as a result of the use of information contained within this document, including, but not limited to, — errors, omissions, or inaccuracies.

www.ingramcontent.com/pod-product-compliance
Lightning Source LLC
Chambersburg PA
CBHW071406210526
45465CB00001B/275